PRAISE FOR JOANNE PALMISANO'S

Salvage Secrets

TRANSFORMING RECLAIMED MATERIALS INTO DESIGN CONCEPTS

"[A]n invaluable first step in the salvage-for-design journey." **—*Fine Homebuilding***

"If you're new to actually *using* salvaged items, like I am, that's where reclaimed material evangelist, designer, and blogger Joanne Palmisano comes in. Her new book, *Salvage Secrets*, is the ultimate guide to getting started. When you finish the book, you'll be armed and ready to search for your own trash-into-treasure find." **—*HGTV, Design Happens***

"Palmisano presents a thorough introduction to the world of salvage design, with just enough practical information to get even a beginner started. Dozens of color photos of interiors that include reclaimed elements help bring the author's points to life . . . . Armed with ideas from the book and some great places to shop (or sift through), you're well on your way to creating a unique, comfortable, earth-friendly home." **—*SuCasa***

"It's a great resource for professional or amateur designers who have a resourceful, green approach to design projects. I would definitely recommend picking it up if you can!" **—www.apartmenttherapy.com**

"I've just seen one of the first copies—and I love it! Joanne demonstrates throughout her book the ease with which recycling and reuse can be incorporated with function and style. Architects, designers, and do-it-yourselfers should all have a copy of this book in their home design library." **—*New England Home***

"Joanne Palmisano offers innovative strategies to transform your interior design ideas in both big and small ways with a little salvage creativity." **—Karin Lidbeck-Brent, Photo Stylist, Producer, and Contributing Editor, *Better Homes and Gardens, Country Living, Good Housekeeping,* and *New England Homes***

"It is an ideal book for anyone considering salvage in design. . . . Often books on design are either practical and plain or only full of photographs with little guidance on how to create the same look in one's own home. *Salvage Secrets* . . . manages to be a design book with both." **—*Portland Book Review***

Salvage Secrets Design & Decor

Salvage Secrets Design & Decor

TRANSFORM YOUR HOME WITH RECLAIMED MATERIALS

Joanne Palmisano

Photographs by Susan Teare

W. W. NORTON & COMPANY · NEW YORK · LONDON

MIX
Paper from responsible sources
FSC® C004791
www.fsc.org

All photos are by Susan Teare, except where otherwise noted in Credits. Illustrations by Cliff Deetjen.

Frontmatter photos: p. 1, see p. 203; p. 2, see p. 168; p. 5, see p. 267; p. 6, see p. 24; p. 8, see p. 210; p. 12, see p. 249; p. 13; see p. 172

Printed in Singapore
FIRST EDITION

For information about permission to reproduce selections from this book, write to Permissions, W. W. Norton & Company, Inc., 500 Fifth Avenue, New York, NY 10110

For information about special discounts for bulk purchases, please contact W. W. Norton Special Sales at specialsales@wwnorton.com or 800-233-4830.

Composition and book design by Kristina Kachele Design, llc
Manufacturing by B&P and KHL Printing Co Pte Ltd
Digital production: Joe Lops
Production Manager: Leeann Graham

Library of Congress Cataloging-in-Publication Data

Palmisano, Joanne.
Salvage secrets design & decor : transform your home with reclaimed materials /
Joanne Palmisano ; photographs by Susan Teare. – First Edition.
pages cm
Includes bibliographical references.
ISBN 978-0-393-73388-4 (pbk.)
1. Salvage (Waste, etc.) in interior decoration. I. Title. II. Title: Salvage secrets design and decor.

NK2115.5.S25P353 2014
747´.1—dc23
2013022291

ISBN 13: 978-0-393-73388-4 (pbk.)

W. W. Norton & Company, Inc., 500 Fifth Avenue, New York, N.Y. 10110
www.wwnorton.com
W. W. Norton & Company Ltd., Castle House, 75/76 Wells St., London W1T 3QT
0987654321

TIM WALKER PICTURES

Contents

Shows
8/17 Great Western @ Burger Night
8/25 Great Western @ Auggiefest '12
8/26 w/ Chris Damon @ Battery Park
9/7 Great Western @ Art Hop
Liberty
Mac
Mac
Sweet 16
Liberty
Mac
Sweet 16

Acknowledgments

First and foremost, this book would not look the way it does without the work of photographer Susan Teare and her team, Lindsay Raymondjack and Toni Finnegan. Susan's extraordinary photography proves just how beautiful salvage can be. Thank you to Cliff Deetjen of Peregrine Design/Build for his architectural drawings. A big thank you to Andrea Dawson, Kevin Olsen, Sara Peterson, Rebecca Shaughnessy, and the entire W. W. Norton publishing team for believing in me once again and making me feel like family. And to copyeditor extraordinaire, Casey Ruble, who helped me to communicate all the stories, secrets, and ideas. I also offer my thanks to my friends Tina Noel, Tawnya Pell, and Shannon Quimby for their constant encouragement and help on my do-it-yourself projects. I am grateful to my parents and siblings, and all my amazing friends who know I'll always love salvage—many of them share my passion. A special thank you goes to my husband, Stephen, and our daughter, Gabrielle, for their unparalleled support. They kept the home fires burning while I was away doing research for this book.

The pursuit of salvage design and decor is an ever-evolving and enlightening journey, and this second *Salvage Secrets* book would not have been possible without the many homeowners, architects, builders, designers, and salvage gurus who gave their support, time, and expertise throughout the writing of the book. Thank you for opening up your homes, businesses, and stores and helping me share your salvage stories. In no particular order, I have listed these individuals (and their companies) here. If I have forgotten you on this list, please forgive me.

Jackie McGilvray of DIY Network; Jessica Helgerson of Jessica Helgerson Interior Design, Yianni Doulis of Yianni Doulis Architecture Studio; Susan Lyon, Tim Wybenga of TVA Architects; Susan and Ryan Hayes; Andy Whitcomb of Whitcomb & Company; Sue Brakeley, Davita Nowland of Nauticals of Marblehead; Patti Moreno and Robert Patton-Spruill of Filmshack; Peter Koeppen of DIY Network; Nancy Ranchel of Replaceinpdx.com; Anne De Wolf of Arciform Design Build; Dana Kirk; Hadley, Dana and Raymond Murphy; Joel Hester of The Weld House; Jane Coslick of Jane Coslick Designs & Restoration; Christopher Twombley of Lounge Lizard; Ryan Gentles; Jane Kim of Jane Kim Design; Barbara and Chris Conner of Conner and Buck Builders; Christine Lobel; George and Rachael Ramos of George Ramos Woodworking; Mary Atwood; Jaclyn Jablkowski of Build It Green!NYC; Teresa Ridlon of Ridlon Interiors; David Ridlon; Michelle de la Vega of Michelle de la Vega Design; Maimei and Hugh Frederick; Colleen Frederick of Studio Frederico; Steve Conant of Conant Metal and Light; Anna Palmer of Refresh Collections; Lori Scotnicki; Renee Tornabene of BulbtoBlossom.com; Kristyn Bester of Arciform DesignBuild; Crystal Shallow of Country Living Magazine; Annette Joseph of Annette Joseph Photostylist; James and Maria Hardison; Nicole Curcio; Bob Jacobs, Nigel Barnes, Justin Grow, Doug Groom, Christopher Cornett, Teresa Holsberry of Rejuvenation; Aaron Danzig, Lisa Jorge De Silva, Gordon Yu, Liz Hoffmire, Sarah Latta and all the great folks at Williams-Sonoma, WSI Designer Marketplace and Cultivate; Chris Munford of Bedrock Industries;

Kerri Hoyt-Pack, Dan, Emma, and Hadley Pack; Stephanie Larrow of Totem Salvaged; Joseph Sassone; Janet Babits, Dave St. Amour, Jeremy Smith and everyone at ReSOURCE; Meghan Spillane; David Knox, Todd Watkins, Brian Barclay of Mason Brothers Architectural Salvage Shop; Kim Rawlins, Katie Hibbs, Stephanie Williams of Sweet Salvage Shop; Rachel Brody of Revolver Salon; Susan Starr, Robert Jolin, Rudolphe Faulcon of Industrie Denim; Kelly LaPlante of Kelly LaPlante Design; Daryl Ross, Michael Barber, Patrick Young of The Bancroft Hotel; Michael Pullen, Jose Billeter of Bamboo Revolution; Matt Higgins and the folks at Coava Coffee Roasters; Kathy Rose of The Store; Ryan Bukstein, Kim Riggs of Ace Hotel; Kim Deetjen, Pamela Picker of TruxCullins Architecture and Interior Design; Stefan Muhle of Casa Madrona Resort and Spa; Anne Quatrano, Selina Clevenger of Abattoir Restaurant; Vivian Bencich of Square Feet Studio; Mike and Jackie Rice of Mt. Hood Bed and Breakfast; Chris Copley, Kevin Owens, Jeff Beer, Molly O'Day of Select Design; Tracee Danyluk of Corkscrew Wine Bar; Leslie Kilgore of Stowe Mountain Lodge; Tricia Rose of Rough Linen; Stefan Sargent; Rosanne Palmisano; Sean Roy; Kelly Giesen of Kelly G Design; Jennifer Siegal of Office of Mobile Design; Shannon Quimby of Shannon Quimby Design/Styling; Glenn and Chase Hoffinger; Robin Cady of Cady Construction; Kim Clements, Joe Schneider of J.A.S. Design Build; Jason Mathews of Jason Mathews Interior Designer and Sheridan & Company; Michael Nielsen; Annie Haviland; Teresa, Terry, Alex and Alexa Hancock; Nathan Good of Nathan Good Architects; Joe Vondrak of Pacific Crest Construction; Patrick and Kelsey Oran; Nathan Patterson; Heather Chontos of Milk Farm Road; Laurie Caswell-Burke; Tim Frost of Peregrine Design Build; Colette Scanlon of This Old House Magazine; Maureen Friedman of Fine Homebuilding Magazine; Tom Cross of Champlain Valley Antiques; Mary Aloi of Vintage Inspired Antiques Marketplace; Karin Lidbeck-Brent of Karin Lidbeck Brent Photostylist; Carol Dupree; Sandy Koepke of Sandy Koepke Interior Design; Dale Emanuel of Goodwill Industries; Laura Takashima of Urban Spruce Design.

Please refer to the Credits at the end of the book for complete design information on each photo.

A big thank you to all those involved!

Burlington
Red Rock Point
South Burlington
Butler Corners

Salvage Secrets Design & Decor

OUR WINDS

◂◂ This unusual, custom-made boat bar was built by Davita Nowland of Nauticals of Marblehead from pieces of a salvaged 1952 Hinckley sailboat. It includes eight fish that represent Susan, the homeowner, and her family. These boat pieces would certainly have been thrown away, but saved and repurposed they create unique nautical furniture pieces. Unique designs, specialized companies, and interesting salvage finds are what give this room character. Everything else is designed around this inventive piece, proving that salvage can be the star of any design.

Introduction

The excited interest generated by my first book, *Salvage Secrets: Transforming Reclaimed Material into Design Concepts*, took me by surprise. I'd always been passionate about using reclaimed material, but it turned out that people all over the country wanted to learn the ins and outs of incorporating one-of-a-kind salvaged items into their homes. I had begun writing the book and creating an accompanying blog with the idea of helping design professionals and interested do-it-yourselfers to feel more comfortable using recycled materials. What I didn't realize was just how great the hunger is for this sort of information.

In the course of visiting and photographing homes for the first book and this one, photographer Susan Teare and I met the most talented, generous, and thoughtful individuals:

homeowners who are so dedicated to recycling that they refuse to use a dumpster when rebuilding an old home from scratch, preferring instead to reuse or repurpose every bit they can; store owners and employees who know and cherish the history of the buildings in which they work; entire companies dedicated to the mindful dismantling of old buildings, creating important jobs along the way; and, finally, homeowners who just want to make a difference.

And so, spurred by this evident enthusiasm and hunger for more, I began to write the book in your hands, *Salvage Secrets Design & Decor*. This book delves into a different way of using reclaimed materials. Whereas my first book addressed the technical considerations of incorporating salvage into your home and concentrated on the materials themselves (stone, concrete, wood, glass, and so on), this book takes a much broader look at the smaller-scale interior design possibilities that salvage can offer, and that anyone can accomplish. The first book explained how to identify a sound slab of wood to use as a rustic accent ceiling beam; this book shows examples of how salvage can be incorporated into design and decor decisions and explains where you can find these treasures.

For those who haven't read my first book, a quick recap: Salvage material goes by many different names. I consider salvage anything that is second-hand: recycled, reclaimed, repurposed, vintage, antique, even "junk." If it's given a chance at a second life, it is all salvage to me.

Many times we may think a piece of wood is too small to save, or that a broken aluminum screen has no value, but I can tell you for a fact—after years of research, traveling, scouting for home decor magazines, and talking to hundreds of people—it isn't and it does. I've seen screens and scraps of plywood transformed into light fixtures, modern sinks, closet panel art, and more. I've seen discarded boat planks transformed into an elegant bar and bed springs made over as candle holders. The possibilities are endless—we just have to know how and where to look for them.

And that's where this book comes in. By displaying a multitude of projects, I will show the huge selection of salvage material available and how it can be used, even if you have no prior experience. You will discover bottle caps that have been turned into backsplashes, old vintage sinks refurbished as kitchen

◂◂ This room makeover was featured in one of the eight videos I did for the DIY NETWORK online video series. Everything is reclaimed—the chandelier, the bedspring candleholders, the marble, the mantel and surround. Even the mirror was a $6 find at a recycle shop. The homeowner found the old metal letter, which is her husband's initial.

▸▸ An old office chair base with a slab of reclaimed lumber atop is now a quaint table that holds some cards and chips for a quick game, as well as recycled canning jars that show off some of the family's waterside treasures. Found at a recycle shop, the chair is an easy place to slip off your shoes and go for a swim. Alone, each of these salvaged and recycled pieces may not look like much, but together they create a casual, welcoming vignette in the home.

centerpieces, a trucking-container-turned-home-addition, an old garage transformed into a house, industrial scuba equipment repurposed as a lamp, furniture created from salvaged wood, and much, much more.

The decorative possibilities of salvage material are as endless as they are unique, and whether you're an interior designer, architect, or other professional seeking inspiration or a do-it-yourself homeowner looking for how-to tips and motivation, my intention with this book is to supply you with loads of great ideas. Take it with you to salvage shops, flea markets, antique shops, and second-hand stores; give it to your builder or architect/designer and point out what you like. My hope is that, as an easy-to-tote paperback, this book will be consulted often and well worn.

To this end, I've made a point of filling these pages with ideas for every budget and style. Taking you room by room, I'll offer a host of salvage design ideas for every space in the house, from kitchens to outdoor areas. If you want specific ideas for a particular room, jump to that chapter; or read all the way through for the full repertoire.

Of course, creative use of reclaimed materials doesn't stop at the private home. Many businesses, large and small, incorporate salvage in their retail and corporate spaces in very innovative ways. Some of my best design ideas have come from the creative displays and functional use of salvage that I've spotted in shopping boutiques, hotels, spas, restaurants, and other places of business. The "retail inspiration" chapter showcases many of these ideas.

Next up is a visual tour and vignettes of fourteen "salvage success stories"—homeowners and designers who have effectively and uniquely used salvaged materials in their design. You'll hear from people who are passionate and creative when it comes to reuse and repurposing, and their efforts may just spur you to create some of your own salvage looks.

Toward the end of the book is a "do-it-yourself with salvage" section that walks you through fun and affordable projects that use easily accessible recycled and salvage material. Invaluable, of course, is the book's final chapter, which will help you discover where you can find the best salvage goods in your own area and across the country. Check out the Resources at the end of the book

This used shipping container sits in the backyard of an urban home and serves as a guest cottage. Designed by the homeowner and the design-build team Arciform, it is a cozy, salvaged getaway for family and friends. You'll see more of the inside of this container throughout the book.

for the names of specific salvage designers, architects, builders, artisans, shops and businesses, and homeowners; in many cases their work is showcased in the book. And speaking of showcasing work, all of these impressive salvage "looks" are beautifully photographed by nationally acclaimed photographer Susan Teare.

In short, the book you have in your hands is the perfect companion for your salvage search, whether you're a novice or seasoned expert. But keep in mind, using salvaged building materials and recycled and repurposed objects isn't just about aesthetics. With almost a third of today's waste generated by the building industry, the choices we make as homeowners or professionals in the industry can mean a great deal. What goes into our homes and where the materials come

from make a huge difference. This was an essential underlying message of my last book, and this book as well.

As one homeowner in my first book stated, “My philosophy of reuse is to encourage people to think about intrinsic values rather than just looks, to know the story of where their house came from and what it will be someday, and to be

The homeowner, Dana, has visited garage sales since she was a little girl, displaying her collection of unique finds throughout her home. On the custom made salvaged wood shelving, along the back wall of her kitchen, she has beautifully styled some of her treasures. Both functional and decorative, they fit perfectly in her sunny Southwest home.

▸▸ Our knowledge of salvage can be passed down and enjoyed by our children. Hadley already appreciates making crafts out of recycled materials. Even the dog, Lola, has a toy made by Sian Keegan out of recycled fabric. The bench is made from reclaimed heart pine, and the wall sconces are recycled champagne flutes custom made by Conant Metal and Light.

aware of their footprint." Respecting the creation of a piece of material or product, whether it is a historic architectural piece or just scrap wood, is important. With this book I hope to express the depth of character of these salvage materials by telling their stories and showing their uniqueness.

When talking about the eco-friendly aspects of using salvage, the concept of supply and demand is key. Using salvaged material in a home or building—or even working it into a piece of furniture, a decorative object, or a fixture—creates a domino effect: More interest in salvage leads to more demand for it and, in turn, more supply. Today, many pieces of salvageable wood, metal, glass—you name it—still end up in the dumpster, burdening our already overtaxed landfills. Whether you use salvage in your design or take the time to drop off your own unwanted materials at a recycling center so someone else can use them, it is a step in the right direction. A study conducted by the National Association of Home Builders estimates that 8,000 pounds of waste are created from the construction of a 2,000 square foot home. If we all do our part, we can drastically reduce that number and help to create jobs in the salvage, recycling, and artisan communities along the way.

I'm thrilled to say that I feel a real change in the air. The builders and homeowners I spoke with during my research for both books not only want to make a difference but also understand and embrace the appeal of salvage design in the home industry. They're actively using salvage as inspiration for their designs. And it's no wonder. The intrinsic value, the history, and the depth of character of salvage pieces are hard to find elsewhere.

And so, I hope this collection of inspirational stories, photos, design ideas, and do-it-yourself projects will help you to rethink salvage and get creative. Let's go!

Where can you find hundreds of bottle caps? Architect Tim Wybenga and his wife, Susan Lyon, asked their friends to save all their discarded bottles caps. With an eye for design, Tim created a pattern, using clear caulk to adhere the caps to a fiberboard. The clean lines of the cabinetry complement the bright and cheerful recycled backsplash.

Joel Hester, owner of The Weld House, is one of many artisans around the globe who make a living building with reclaimed material. The Weld House started as a side business to Joel's job with a small welding company making bed frames. Now, working full-time (and employing others as well), and with bigger and better equipment, Joel is creating steel furniture made from old cars and trucks. His pieces range from coffee tables (see Chapter 3) to full bars. Each is one-of-a-kind.

Designer Jane Coslick is well known in Tybee Island, Georgia, as the designer who not only dares to use bright colors but is also unafraid of salvaged, reclaimed, and vintage pieces. On her large sun porch, only steps from the water, she enjoys a cozy reading area with upholstered chairs she found at flea markets and second-hand shops and then slip-covered in fabric with bold patterns. Vintage dressers were painted in Caribbean colors and the coffee table is part of an old boat.

A colored glass display at the store Lounge Lizard, in Portland, Oregon. Midcentury glass is just one of hundreds of salvaged, second-hand, or recycled items that you can easily add to your home's decor.

This New York City contemporary penthouse apartment, remodeled by Jane Kim Design and interior designer Ben Shulman, is filled with reclaimed wood. The contrast between the modern, gray lacquer cabinets and the rough-hewn walls, which are made of reclaimed hemlock barn wood, is stunning, proving that old and new can mix nicely. Beams of heart pine, reclaimed from a previous job site by the contractor, were de-nailed and re-sawn for the kitchen island. The top of the island is from thicker cuts of the same wood, finished with polyurethane. The open shelving, of the same reclaimed wood as the walls and ceiling, blends well with the paneling and is mitered into the wall with steel L-brackets. The open space, warm tones of the salvage wood, and stained concrete floors make for easy entertaining in a comfortable green environment—just what the homeowner wanted.

Kitchens & Dining Rooms

KITCHENS

Whether you're building from scratch, remodeling, or just adding accessories, it's important to first decide how you want to use your kitchen. Do you tend to keep a laptop or iPad on the kitchen island? If so, maybe a small space for a kitchen desk would be useful. Do you find yourself often eating in the kitchen because a wall separates it from the dining room? Maybe it's time to take the wall down and add some salvaged beams to give a visual and structural separation. Would you prefer the ease of open shelving so you don't have to keep opening a cabinet for a glass? Would reconfiguring the cabinets beneath the sink give

▸▸ This kitchen and dining-area remodel involved repainting all the cabinetry, hanging vintage lights over the island and dining table, reupholstering two chairs with second-hand material, and adding a vintage dining table. The retro collection of bar ware and accessories offers a good pop of color. With just a few simple changes, including repainting the cabinetry instead of replacing it, this space went from an outdated 1980s look to one that feels modern, hip, and happy.

you a bigger, more convenient place for your recycling and compost? Planning ahead will help you create a design that fits your needs, enhances efficiency, and appeals to your sense of style. If you're remodeling, it also will help you figure out what you can recycle from the old kitchen and what you can add that is salvaged, vintage, or antique.

Flooring

Amazing kitchen floors can be created with salvage material in hundreds of different ways. Of course, most people like to stick to wood, tiles, concrete, or similar materials for ease of cleaning and the non-slip factor—rarely do you see a wall-to-wall rug in these areas—but that doesn't mean a wonderful vintage or salvage area rug or upcycled carpet remnant won't look great, perhaps under a moveable island or as a runner near the sink. Once you have a feel for what kind of flooring you want, you can start your salvage search.

Easiest to find are reclaimed wood options, concrete with recycled aggregate (fly ash or glass), recycled cement tile, and recycled bricks. Hundreds of companies, easily found on the Internet, sell and create these materials throughout the country, making it simple to find one near you. And another benefit: Many of these products can be custom made or finished to your exact style.

If you already have a wood floor, but it's dated or worn, you can change the look of it instead of replacing it. Many homeowners don't think a dark stain will work on their floors, but I've seen some dated white oak turn into a rich espresso color in a flash, transforming the entire feel of the kitchen. Another way of handling old floors is to paint them either a cottage color—grays, greens, or blues—or give them a checkered pattern for a vintage kitchen look. Will they scratch? Possibly, but by using floor and porch

DESIGN TIP

Remodeling your kitchen? Don't start ripping everything out without first having a plan. Can the cabinets be left in place and simply painted or refaced? If not, can you use them in the laundry room or the kids' playroom? Reusing your own materials is the best way to salvage. And even if you can't use them, remember that someone else can! If you're getting rid of a nice architectural piece, an architectural salvage shop will pay you something for it. You can list it on Craigslist or another online site (although you'll have to deal with strangers coming to your house). Recycle centers are another option. You can drop your stuff off or pay a fee for pickup—and even if you do pay for pickup, you'll still get the donation value and won't have to spend a fortune on dump fees. (Plus, recycling is much better for the environment.) Don't underestimate what can be recycled—pretty much everything has another life in it. Salvaged sinks, lights, countertops, cabinets—these are just the beginning of a kitchen you'll love, use, and live in.

Monday Tues Wed Thurs Fri
Salmon Pasta Bagels
Saturday Sunday
Bath - Oliver
Floors - mom
Laundry Leo
Kitchen Dad

paints and with a proper seal they will last much longer with very few touch-ups over the years. Follow the advice of a floor refinisher, including doing the upfront work of sanding, and you can repurpose your existing floors without removing a thing.

When starting with a new structure or remodeling, reclaimed wood is a great choice. It is easy to find and the look and feel cannot be duplicated with new lumber. Reclaimed wood is one of the most popular salvaged material on the market today—it can be found everywhere, and more and more businesses are dismantling buildings that have gorgeous old wood and bringing it back to you in the marketplace. Also, many kinds of wood once frequently used in old buildings—chestnut, oak, old-growth redwood, heart of pine—are now almost impossible to get as new lumber (especially at wide widths) because those tree species are either protected, restricted, endangered, or less abundant than they once were. Old wood from decommissioned buildings is likely from old growth forests, not tree farms. Wood from old growth forests grows at a slower rate than on tree farms, giving it a tighter grain so it's hard as nails and has loads of character. (Another reason to recycle our materials instead of putting them in the dumpster.) And some of the woods we had in the past are now completely unavailable as new lumber—we must help preserve their presence in our lives and our homes.

DESIGN TIP

If you're building new, think "old." Reclaimed lumber or salvaged tile can be used for the floors and cabinets; recycled glass is perfect for lighting or tiling. Even concrete countertops can be made with up to 85% recycled material—whether it's glass or fly ash. Vintage sinks—cast iron, porcelain, slate, soapstone, and more—are in abundance at architectural salvage shops or online. Review your design and think about what you can use that is either salvaged or made from recycled material. If you are buying something new, then think about its future—is it built to last? Can it be recycled? Some research suggests that creating products from recycled materials uses up to 98% less energy than producing them from new material.

Concrete and tile floors can have a significant amount of recycled material in them. The added benefit of concrete is that it's incredibly durable—and, in the unlikely case that it needs to be removed, it can be recycled again. Concrete was once considered just a subfloor material, but when it's the main structural floor of the house, carpet or new wood flooring does not necessarily need to be added on top, saving money and the need for additional raw materials. Plus, salvaged materials added to concrete mix can offer a thousand different looks: Recycled fly ash gives concrete the appearance of stone; recycled glass crushed into a

Concrete with recycled aggregate is just one type of kitchen-floor option. The floor of this sunny modern home, created by Vermont Eco-Floors, is filled with local aggregate. Instead of crushing the aggregate into a powder for a stone-like look, many of the salvaged pieces were kept large so they could be seen by the naked eye, giving the floor a flecked appearance.

powder can also give the appearance of stone; or, with a natural dye, you can achieve a bright, colorful look. Large chunks of glass or local stone aggregate provide a variety of textured looks. Non-toxic dyes and sealers can be used to finish the concrete, whether you want a matte surface or a highly polished one that reflects light. Add radiant heat to your recycled concrete or tile floor and you have a modern, energy-efficient salvaged product for any style home.

DESIGN TIP

Concrete not made with recycled aggregate uses only cement—a very energy-intensive product thought to cause about 6% of the world's carbon dioxide emissions. Ask your builder, designer, or architect about companies that use salvage material as the aggregate or filler. These concretes are eco-friendly and are a strong and stable product for flooring, sinks, and countertops.

This island top is made from 85% recycled copper and salvaged boards (underneath the copper). Of all metals, copper is among those with the most recycled content. The vintage corbels used as brackets, sealed to prevent flaking, were found at Mason Brothers Architectural Salvage in Vermont. The sides of the island are from old doors collected by the homeowner—they not only gave the island a whole new look but also helped enlarge it to make room for a trash bin and more shelving on the other side. This project was featured in one of the eight DIY NETWORK videos that feature my salvage design work.

Countertops

Countertops are not only one of the first things you see in a kitchen but they play a key role in your comfort and the function of your space. Whether you are baking bread or wanting to make sure your guests are comfortable at your kitchen island, you need to choose countertop and island top materials wisely. Are they used for cooking tasks as well as seating and eating? If so, make sure the materials you select are appropriate. My kitchen island top is made from the salvaged wood of 1880s railroad trusses that are just lightly sanded with coats of polyurethane, while my counters are pieces of soapstone tile (many salvaged from a discard pile). I entertain and eat on the island but I cook, cut, and chop at the counters, knowing full well that my island wood could not take that amount of abuse.

So many different style possibilities can be achieved. Second-hand metal countertops from a restaurant-supply shop will give you a clean,

modern look. Highly polished, wide, reclaimed wood planks are perfect for a more "French countryside" feel. For a contemporary aesthetic, salvaged pieces of 24x24-inch stone tile can be picked up at your local stone company or found through local online sites like Craigslist. A laminated top, dropped off at your local rebuild center, will give you an eclectic, retro look, and an old-world feel can be achieved by a butcher block top made from recycled wood—ask your local builder to put one together for you. And don't forget about concrete counters made with recycled content.

The extra-thick concrete countertops are made with recycled glass aggregate, and the wood countertop and beams are from salvaged trees that were cleared from the property for the home site and dried and milled locally. The vintage area rug is a great example of how you can add warmth to a stone floor. Even a new home can incorporate salvage in the structure and decor.

Cabinetry and Shelving

If you are remodeling, you can choose to repurpose or reface your original cabinetry. Sometimes simply applying a new coat of paint is sufficient. An array of colors and finishes are on the market today. For wood cabinets a good sanding, a coat of primer, and a great acrylic or chalk paint will do. For laminated cabinets, a little more work with a more heavy duty spray paint might work best. If you're not sure, bring a cabinet door in to your paint store and ask them to advise you as to the best approach to repurposing. You might not even think of turning old dark wood into a bright blue or a crisp white. If the cabinet doors are beyond repair or embellishment, replace them with new ones. For a bolder change, remove the doors and make open shelving. Don't forget to donate the old doors to your local salvage shop!

Making new cabinets out of salvaged wood is another option, although finding gorgeous pieces of recycled lumber for finished-looking cabinetry is a bit trickier than it is for flooring. Cabinetry wood needs to have less bow, because it is not being held down by nails, and fewer knots, because they affect the finish. Finding a cabinetmaker or builder who specializes in old wood cabinetry is usually your best bet.

Rustic, paneled, painted—these are all options when using old wood. Salvaged-wood cabinetry doesn't have to look old or even have a natural wood color—you can paint it white or even a bright color for a more modern effect. For a more rustic look, try prefinished cabinetry made out of a funkier wood material. Many builders and do-it-yourselfers use recycled pallets and old barn paneling, leaving the rough texture and weathered grayish color as is. Surrounding an island or re-facing the front of cabinetry doors with this kind of wood (paint the back of the cabinet doors white) will give you a nice French-farmhouse look.

Learn about the quality of the reclaimed wood you are considering and you get a better idea of where and how to use it. Some wood is great for flooring but too thin for a good island top; or perfect for wall planking but not structurally sound enough to serve as an exposed beam running through the kitchen. Wood experts, salvage-shop owners, and other professionals can help you navigate the wood or scrap pile. This piece of butcher block was made from dozens of species of wood, with some pieces as narrow as a quarter inch.

◂◂ You can pull together a stunning kitchen by deciding on the salvage pieces you want to use and then designing around them. This kitchen design features a reclaimed-wood butcher-block island top; old door panels that wrap around the island; painted, recycled dimensional lumber for the floor; an architectural salvaged sink; salvaged piping and vintage worker lamps on cords; recycled metal hardware; second-hand faucets and appliances; and even a kitchen-cabinet set found online.

Reclaimed wood is easy to find, but wood from your own property works, too. Salvaging trees from a construction site is a great—and efficient—first step in reusing material you already have. This bar-height countertop, which separates the kitchen area from the dining room, is reclaimed pine from the property itself. When the family had to clear some of the land for the house, they felt strongly about reusing the wood, which they dried and had locally milled. They left the tree's natural living edge on the slab, and kept the splits as well. The character of the wood itself is the design.

▸▸ The unique tiling in this townhouse kitchen was highlighted with vintage brackets. Flush with the modern stove hood, the brackets add texture and depth to the basic structure. Structural design details like these—as well as layers of details like the vintage scale, wall basket, lamp, and silver vessel for holding large utensils—take townhouse design to another level, filling the home with character and warmth.

Dinner
6pm
sweet kitchen

◀ ▲ In these two kitchens, the same salvaged wood was used to very different effect. George Ramos, a woodworker and cabinetmaker, used reclaimed Douglas fir from an old Port of Portland building. For his own galley-style kitchen (left), he painted the reclaimed wood white. For a client's kitchen (above), he left the natural warm tones of the fir and finished it with OSMO Wax Finish. Both kitchens use recycled glass in the cabinets as well.

Buying recycled or salvaged cabinetry is also an option. Rebuild centers stockpile large quantities of old cabinetry. You can go over them with a fine-tooth comb, checking for damage on the corners and making sure everything opens correctly. Remember, when cabinets are not attached to a wall, their structure may be skewed a little—consult with your builder or the rebuild center to get a better feel for the cabinetry.

Most joints and corners can be repaired, but defects like cracks down the middle and serious water damage are harder to fix. Check whether the cabinetry is solid wood (usually more expensive) or laminate. Laminate is harder to fix. Also, be aware that particleboard is made of sawdust and glue—get it near water (around a sink) and it will surely fall apart. Another question is whether the wood is dovetailed or stapled together. Dovetailed is the way to go—good dovetailed joints at the corners are a sign of quality construction. Plastic joints or staples are not as good. Weigh all the pros and cons. A solid

Shopping at the Build It Green!NYC shop in Brooklyn, I came across an entire recycled modern-style kitchen set with contemporary hardware already on it. It could be inserted into a kitchen as is, or it could be painted a bold color, like a bright Caribbean blue, to change the look but not the style. Add a countertop of salvaged stone or butcher block and you have an instant kitchen.

wood piece, for example, may cost more upfront but require less maintenance and risk of replacement in the future.

Once you have a basic understanding of your cabinetry choices—repurposing your existing cabinets, making new ones from high-end reclaimed wood, buying recycled cabinetry, or taking on a do-it-yourself project out of old wood and brackets, you will be able to piece together a cabinetry arrangement for your home. The right recycled and salvaged pieces may be a little more difficult to find than new wood, but it can be more affordable and, even when it's not, certainly more stunning and eco-friendly.

Some of the most exciting salvage discoveries are full kitchen inserts. These become available when people renovate their entire kitchen and—thankfully—donate or sell the insert to a salvage shop or list it online and ask you to pick it up. For anywhere from $500 to $5000, you can have an entire kitchen plopped down in your home. I've seen architectural salvage shops with entire 1950s-era mod kitchens, complete with metal cabinets and swirly-patterned Formica countertops. Don't like the color of the metal? Easy! Take it to your local car refinisher and have them sandblast and repaint it. Unique and ready to go—just pull up a truck.

Freestanding furniture, such as old pine cupboards, baker's racks, and vintage butcher blocks, are a wonderful way to add character and storage to your kitchen (see photo on the next page). They're also often more affordable than built-in pieces, and you can take them with you if you move in the future.

Open shelving—as opposed to cabinetry—is the hot new trend in kitchen design. Open shelves not only allow easier access to cookware but also can be used to show off brightly colored vintage dishes and glasses. Another plus is that they are easy to install, require less material to make, and are usually more affordable than custom cabinetry.

For a strong design statement, try using salvaged wood as a wainscoting behind the shelves and painting the shelves a bright color. Metal office shelves can give your kitchen a clean, industrial look; glass placed on old brackets will lend a more country feel. Boxes pushed together instantly create a whole wall of shelves.

DESIGN TIP

Vintage corbels make great brackets, but be aware that many of them were made for porches and they are not at a 90-degree angle. If the ones you pick out aren't level, see if there's a way to adjust them with a shim (which can be hidden by painting over the bracket after the shim is added). Also, double-check that they are structurally sound, especially if they are a structural part of your design.

Antique baker's or shoe racks, pie cupboards, industrial shelving—these are just a few of the freestanding pieces you can add to your kitchen. Interior designer Teresa Ridlon uses an old baker's rack for additional storage in her own kitchen. Filled with vintage jars and baskets, it's both useful and visually appealing. The old metal basket on the floor and the vintage sewing table give the kitchen a French country look. Seeing the wall through the shelving makes the kitchen seem bigger and more open, a perfect solution for smaller spaces like apartments or cottages.

When considering your shelving options, first figure out what you intend to store on them. If they're going to hold your heavy coffee machine and toaster, they'll need to be wider than a normal pantry shelf and secured into a stud in the wall. Also, if you're working with older metal brackets additional holes may need to be put in them—a pretty easy job for a metalworker or a handy do-it-yourselfer.

Sinks

Sinks, appliances, and even shelving can be found in a variety of locations. A porcelain-enameled cast-iron farmhouse sink can be found at an architectural salvage shop, a rebuild center, or even on Craigslist. An industrial-sized stainless steel sink can be found at a second-hand restaurant-supply center or even a school changing out its fixtures. You can also get more recently made sinks at a rebuild center—many have hundreds of cast-iron and metal sinks from the 70s, 80s, and 90s in their yards. Some may be too small or shallow for use in a kitchen but perfect for a bar-top sink or even a funky bathroom sink.

Other salvaged sink options are stone, such as a vintage soapstone, or even those old concrete laundry sinks that many homes used to have in the basement. These older sinks are best when they have been water-tested or even re-glued. Soapstone companies sometimes sell vintage sinks, or you can find them online or at salvage shops. If they don't have any, ask them to look for you. With stone sinks, it's important to know your dimensions before shopping—and to keep the design open until you find the right sink. Stone sinks are heavy and need more structural support than a simple aluminum or metal sink. Also, some are very deep and you may not be able to put full cabinets or even a garbage disposal under it—so, again, plan ahead.

The depth of a salvaged sink is as important as its length and width. Brooklyn's Build It Green!NYC shop has an abundance of sinks. Finding an extra-deep one may take a little bit of searching, but you'll discover one eventually if you visit a salvage shop often enough. Some of these centers are now taking pictures of their products and posting them online. Join their email list to receive updates.

Several unique salvage features went into this tiny kitchen in the Seattle home of interior designer Michelle de la Vega. The oversized sink—originally from a local school and found at Second Use in Seattle—is a big-statement piece. By highlighting such a functional piece, Michelle was able to keep the rest of the space open and simple, making it feel bigger than it is. Built around the salvaged sink is open shelving made with salvaged wood and brackets also found at the Second Use shop. The countertop tiles are returns that Michelle found in the discount pile at a tile shop. Along with the vintage industrial light over the sink, the many vintage and reclaimed appliances and accessories—including the old metal lunchbox and toaster—round off the kitchen's modern industrial look.

Appliances

More and more energy-efficient stoves, microwaves, and refrigerators can be found at rebuild centers that carry appliances. Many of these centers have repair shops and make sure the equipment is working properly before they even put it on the floor. Second-hand pieces may need to be rewired for safety, and some can even be changed to improve efficiency. Even vintage pieces, like those coveted, enamel-covered stoves from the 1950s, can be rewired or repaired. Most local stove-repair professionals can handle such jobs, and parts are still available online or at restoration hardware shops.

Lighting

Ambient, accent, decorative, and task lighting—plus, of course, the ever-important natural light—are the types of lighting you should consider in kitchen design. Often, one fixture can be used for multiple lighting types. A task light, for example, can also be a decorative piece, as can an ambient or accent light. Where you need the light, how it will reflect in the room, and the way it makes you feel are all important.

When considering how to light the sink and countertop area, task lighting is important. Recessed lights are popular (and can be found at rebuild centers) and by swapping in a vintage fixture for one of them—perhaps over the sink—you can add character to your room while maintaining its functionality.

Some of the most common light fixtures you see above kitchen islands are pendant lights. Many artisans are creating pendant lighting with old wire industrial baskets, or you can try recycled bubble glass to achieve a vintage look. Pick up some old brass chandeliers, spray paint them a bright color, and hang a few over your island for a quick and easy DIY project.

Think about how lighting fixtures can serve as statement pieces in your kitchen without competing with one another (or with the fixtures in your dining room, if yours is an open floor plan). Decide on the type of light you need—task, mood, pendant, or statement piece—then imagine what salvaged materials could create each of them.

DESIGN TIP

Think canned vegetables, coffee, soup, spaghetti sauce, and pet food, and you'll get an idea of how much steel is out there today. And that's just in the grocery store—let's not forget the building trades. If you recycle steel cans and use materials from recycled steel, you do the world a lot of good. Every little piece of steel can be scrapped, melted down, and reformed—a process that takes much less energy (in fact, about 75% less!) than does making a product from virgin material. You can make countertops, lighting fixtures, sinks and hardware from recycled metal. Or you can use the steel cans or barrels themselves to create one-of-a-kind designs.

This remodeled kitchen includes an island made from reclaimed heart of pine and two extra-large pendant lights that used to be in a school gymnasium. The pendant lights were found and repurposed by Conant Metal and Light, a specialty lighting company that creates unique fixtures out of old salvaged material.

Hardware and More

When we think about kitchen hardware, we think drawer handles, pulls, and knobs, but modern kitchens include a few more details. Built-in drain boards and trash, recycling, and compost receptacles are being integrated into today's kitchen designs. Salvaged baskets are one option; vintage metal drainers or even new ones made with salvaged metal are another. Hardware is a great way to add a unique salvage touch. Mismatched vintage pieces, modern pieces custom made from 100% recycled aluminum, and colorful recycled-glass pulls are just a few of the many possibilities.

This concrete counter and sink, made with recycled aggregate, offer another fine example of how salvaged and recycled products can be used to achieve a contemporary look with a modern function. The metal drain board, made with recycled material, is built into the concrete counter and can be slid over the sink.

The reclaimed American-walnut floors that butt up against the concrete kitchen floor provide a nice separation of this space. The picnic-table-style dining set is from Barntiques, a Pennsylvania company that creates rough-hewn furnishings from century-old barn wood. And the recessed shelving in the living room (background) is from the same reclaimed wood as that used in the kitchen.

DINING ROOMS

More and more, in today's new homes and remodels, the dining area is a part of the kitchen. Whether the table is actually in the kitchen or next to it in an open room, the two spaces are now usually considered the same, one flowing easily into the other.

Whether you want a high-end antique dining set with a recognizable name, a sleek midcentury black-and-chrome set, or quirky mismatched chairs around a picnic table, your dining room can be created entirely out of salvaged material. Your dining area should reflect the style of the rest of your home, especially if you have an open floor plan. It's okay to have a traditional home with modern touches or even an eclectic look, but the space needs to have a smooth visual flow. Pick out your salvaged pieces with this in mind and your design will pull together easily.

◂◂ This open-air kitchen and dining space work well for an active family. Cabinetry recycled from an old school and vintage lighting (including an old school light) from School House Lighting are two of the many salvaged design elements. Colleen, the homeowner, also collects old glassware and dishes. The bar stools are from a second-hand store; Colleen repainted them in a lime green to contrast with the red wall. The inside stools she found in a dumpster. Bartering with a contractor got them the SlateScape counter. An overhead double-hung window, hanging from a chain on the porch ceiling, is a great example of what you can do with recycled modern-style windows (or a garage door). The porch ceiling is also a mixture of painted salvaged boards.

▸ These two very different dining rooms demonstrate that reclaimed wood can be any style you want. The salvaged farmhouse table with sideboard and wood benches work well in the more traditional home (above). The custom-made, cafe-style eating area (right), made from reclaimed wood from the homeowner's property, is perfect in this more clean-lined contemporary home.

▸▸ To make the small dining area feel light and airy, interior designer Michelle de la Vega, the owner, added a full glass door she picked up second-hand. Next to it, serving as a tiny entrance table, is an old industrial-shop cabinet she found on the side of the road. It holds a vintage school clock. The dining table is made from old wood and has a concrete base. The folding chairs are from Goodwill—Michelle spray-painted them orange—and the highly collectible, Atomic-Age Emeco bar stools were found at a yard sale for only $15 each. Michelle fashioned the light fixture above the dining table out of a metal pan and a piece of pipe. The wicker clamshell-shaped chair she picked up on Craigslist. Simple yet stunning, this room shows how a variety of salvage materials from an array of places can be mixed and matched for a comfortable, eclectic style.

Flooring and Rugs

The flooring in a dining space is often more decorative than what you'll find in a kitchen. Made of salvaged tile or reclaimed wood, covered with an extra-large vintage rug or left bare, a floor can tell a great story.

Salvaged wood in a dining room can have a herringbone pattern or be end cut, inlayed, whitewashed, distressed, or even painted in a pattern to look like a rug. If you're adding an actual rug, it's usually best to stick to wools that are more stain-resistant. Vintage Oriental and Persian rugs are classics, but more modern rugs with bold patterns are becoming increasingly popular. Even just a carpet remnant will feel good underfoot, add another texture, and serve as a great sound absorber. As a rule of thumb, most rugs under a dining table extend 5 feet beyond the width of the table on all sides. Look for salvaged rugs in your local paper, your front porch forum, or at an antique fair. Know the size and shape you need, as well as the amount you want to pay, before you head off (and don't forget to add in the carpet-cleaning fee).

Tables and Chairs

What does your space require? Do you need a 6-foot table or will that be too tight in your dining area? (Remember to allow 3 feet on all sides from walls or cabinets for mobility, if you can.) What kind of style will look best in your home? Second-hand tables are great because they are usually pretty easy to find. Start locally by checking out the antique shops or vintage and second-hand shops that specialize in midcentury merchandise, or find a woodworker who makes tables. Rebuild centers that carry furniture will have many tables from the 70s and 80s. If you're looking for a bargain, you can sometimes start there. But many of those tables are not made of solid wood—they're laminate, which makes them harder to sand and paint. Make sure you know what you're getting into before you purchase anything. Is it solid wood? Does the veneer have scratches and are they repairable? Is the table wobbly just because one of the legs needs to be screwed in tighter? These are pretty easy fixes, especially if you are a handy do-it-yourselfer.

If you can't find what you want, have a table made out of salvaged wood instead. Many companies specialize in custom-made salvaged wood tables; ask

Everybody is a genius.

It can be hard to find a set of four or six chairs, so when I see them—like at this rebuild center in Brooklyn—I like to snap them up, especially when they have a more contemporary design. If there's a name on the chair (usually on the underside), I look it up. Sometimes the shop owner will know the maker even if the chairs aren't marked.

your local salvage shop for a recommendation. If you are handy and want to build one yourself check out my step-by-step video on the DIY NETWORK, *How to Build a Farmhouse Table Out of Salvaged Wood*, for an overview.

Style and shape are other considerations for tables and chairs. Round, picnic-table style, folding, and corner bench are just a few options for table shapes; styles range from cottage to modern, traditional to contemporary, rustic to retro. Once you decide on a style, shape, and size, you can begin brainstorming about where to find it or where to have it made.

Let's not forget name brands and popular collectibles. I'm the first to redo, upcycle, repurpose, and repaint, but there are times when none of these options is appropriate. Certain antique, vintage, and second-hand pieces are considered collector-quality and are highly coveted—altering them in any way can significantly reduce their value. So before you reupholster, paint, or even sand and refinish, look at the furnishing to find out if it was made by a well-known designer. Gustav Stickley is considered the leader in the American Craftsman style; Paul Evans is known for his midcentury modern work. Charles Eames, Chippendale, and Emeco are other important names—the list goes on and on. If your piece does turn out to be a collectable, it's best to consult a professional who specializes in that designer's work. He or she can point you to someone who can restore the piece without compromising its value.

◂◂ A vintage Stickley set, found at a local antique shop for a great price, gives a traditional look to this dining area overlooking a lake. Although it was not made by Gustav himself (those are highly coveted and sometimes can go for hundreds of thousands of dollars), the dining set is still high quality, made by Stickley's company, and can be passed down from generation to generation.

Creating an atmosphere with a specific object is important in salvage design. The owner of this Southwest home did just that in her dining room. With extra-high ceilings and open space in her kitchen and dining rooms, she needed big-statement pieces to make the space work. She picked up the vintage table at Indus, Phoenix's largest supplier of Old World and rustic furnishings. The lighting fixture she saw at a regular consignment shop, just lying on the floor. She brought it home, had it rewired, added the unique chain (spray-painting it to match the fixture), and hung it over the table.

Lighting

Lighting is one of the most important aspects of your dining room. Ambience lighting is more important here than task lighting is. Whether it's natural light or created through ceiling fixtures, wall sconces, or table or floor lamps, lighting sets the mood of the room. Lighting structures are one of the easiest salvaged materials to find, and there are hundreds of different styles, from elaborate antique chandeliers to funky midcentury modern swag lamps. You can also have a piece custom made from salvaged material, or make one yourself if you're a creative, handy type. Whatever the style, the goal is to be able to dim the light to soften the lines in the room. Picking out the right bulbs is also important—some bulbs throw a warm light whereas others are cool. And make sure you don't go over the wattage limit for the fixture.

In this dining area, the homeowner decided to go bold with her colors. Second-hand chairs reupholstered in bright blues and yellows surround a vintage oak pedestal table, the only traditional piece in the room. The brass chandelier and wall sconces were painted lime green, giving them an entirely different appearance and lending a more retro look to the room. Candle bulbs on a dimmer keep the lighting in the room soft and glowing. The glasses and pitcher on the table are from the homeowner's online company, which sells vintage bar collections.

◂ Salvage ideas abound in designer Jane Coslick's all-in-one office cottage-kitchen-and-dining area. Retro metal cabinets, an old cast-iron sink with two drain boards, and a uniquely layered painted vintage oak pedestal table are just a few of the highlights. The mix and match of second-hand chairs, including the reupholstered side chair, with more modern ones creates an inviting space. The vintage dishware and accessories are kept simple and are in keeping with the casual cottage vibe of Tybee Island, Georgia.

◂◂ The Lounge Lizard, a second-hand shop in Portland, Oregon, has hundreds of retro lighting fixtures for every room in the house. Unique lighting will liven up any space, especially if it contrasts with an entirely different look, like a traditional table or rough-hewn wood.

Designer Jane Coslick's cottage home, which is only steps to the beach, is bright and happy. Using part of an antique carousal as a headboard, she designed her bedroom with pops of color and fun. A second-hand desk and bench are painted blue, with a contrasting zebra pattern on the seat. Sitting on the desk is a vintage three-piece mirror, as well as a repurposed lamp made from an old trophy. A salvaged piece of green board, with old hooks added on, serves as a great place for Jane to hang bags or beach towels. All the doors in the cottage are antique, and each is painted a different color—this one (reflected in the mirror) in a pretty pink. Old shutters on the inner wall window allow for ventilation while still giving Jane privacy in the bedroom. No matter what weather is coming off the ocean outside, the interior of this cottage, with all its salvaged finds, is sunny all day.

Bedrooms & Bathrooms

BEDROOMS

Bedrooms are a special place in the house—private spaces where you go to relax, read, and rest comfortably. And because they have fewer functional requirements than some other rooms, like the kitchen, they afford more flexibility in design. Light and airy or dark and cavelike, sparse and simple or filled with antiques and layers of textures and textiles—a bedroom can be designed in whatever style suits you. And whether you want a simple space with nothing distracting a good night's sleep or a cozy safe haven chock full of mementos, salvage can help you create the perfect room.

Flooring

Bedrooms are pretty standard when it comes to designing floors. Wood and rugs are the most common materials, making it easy to use salvaged material. Salvaged wood floors (in their natural state or painted) can be accompanied by a large area rug for a layer of texture as well as for warmth and comfort under bare feet on a cool night.

Large vintage rugs can be found at antique shops, specialty rug shops, or online. Another option is to create your own area rug out of a piece of carpet remnant or paint a plain rug you already have (see Chapter 7). Wall-to-wall carpeting can be achieved with recycled material as well—you can purchase carpet squares (like the ones at the Bancroft Hotel, featured in Chapter 5, Retail Inspiration) or full roll-out carpet made with recycled materials like old soda bottles.

Many companies make recycled carpets with hundreds of patterns and colors to choose from. Some are made from recycled plastic bottles or textiles, and others are made from old carpet pieces and rugs. Flor, for example, a popular brand, carries high-end designer carpet squares made from recycled materials. Mohawk makes their EverStrand line out of plastic bottles (turned into chips then into fiber thread and then into carpets) diverting millions of bottles from our landfills. The Carpet Recyclers take old carpets and make an array of new products out of them, including—you guessed it—carpets and carpet pads. These are just a few examples of the hundreds of companies that are helping make a change in how we use recycled products. Recycled flooring options are everywhere; you just have to get creative in finding them and choosing the option that fits your needs.

DESIGN TIP

When you are working with salvaged wood, whether you found it drifting in the ocean or stashed in someone's shed, you should take the time to scrub it with a wire brush and remove any nails, screws, or staples that could get caught in your cutting tools. Then wash it well (if it's painted, follow lead-paint removal guidelines or contact a certified contractor to remove it). If you decide to keep the old paint on any wood pieces, make sure to seal it with a polyurethane or similar product to keep it from flaking. Worried about insects? Some wood treatments, such as borate, can be sprayed on to help protect against bugs. Last but not least, let the wood dry completely before you use it. You can do this by leaving it outside in a dry area (remember to turn the wood often) or you can use a kiln. Drying the wood will also help rid it of insects, especially if you use a kiln. If there are still some punky (soft) spots, you'll need to cut them out or reconsider the piece, especially if you plan to use it structurally.

Walls

Paneling, wainscoting, shelving, bookcases, recycled fiberboard paneling, vintage wallpapers, tiles—these are a few of the salvage options for bedroom walls. By using reclaimed floorboards or creating a horizontal panel effect with varied widths and styles of trim, you can make your space as serene, romantic, or intense as you want.

If you want to keep the walls themselves simple, add bold salvaged decor, such as vintage quilts, which are an easy way to cover a large area without deal-

With the help of her brother, the owner of this country home, Lori Scotnicki, created a wall closet that not only handles all her clothing-storage needs but looks great as well. Using fallen tree branches from a friend's house, they cut the pieces with a band saw and then dried them in the oven for 4 hours at a low temperature. Then Lori sanded them, hand-placed them onto the storage unit her brother built, and finished the piece with linseed oil. It was a time-consuming process, but she's pleased with the results. The salvaged floors are a mix of pine and spruce from an old barn, and they run throughout the house.

DESIGN TIP

Wood reclaimed from old warehouses, grain buildings, homes, barns, and outbuildings typically come in the form of planks. The most common types are tongue-and-groove, shiplap, and butt-jointed. Whatever the type, the planks can be used as is, re-cut into strips, or otherwise changed to fit your building requirements. To get a feel for the color of the wood, slightly sand down a piece then wet it to see what it would look like with a finish. This will remove the patina produced by dirt and weathering, which often turn the wood gray or even black.

A full wall unit made with salvaged material can be an entire bedroom design. This design uses salvaged wood to create a cottage feel by including the bed, shelving, and headboard as a single unit. Building cabinetry as part of the bed frame, especially in a small bedroom, gives the room style and functionality at the same time. The salvaged dimensional lumber (2x2, 2x4, and 1x4), placed in a wainscoting pattern, gives the unit texture and depth. A couple of vintage desk lamps mounted as wall sconces add to the charm.

◂ This clever wall art was made from neckties picked up at a Phoenix second-hand shop. The side-by-side British and American flags give the impression of a headboard and anchor the space.

▴ This contemporary home of architect Tim Wybenga and his wife, Susan, is filled with fabulous design ideas, including the paneled walls and doors on sliders. Tim used Homasote (a brand name for wall boards made from recycled newsprint) to create the look. Cut into the recycled boards in creative circular shapes are his grandfather's old slides from botanist presentations in the Netherlands. The chair in the bedroom once belonged to Susan's grandmother; Susan had it reupholstered and painted. The flower artwork is Tim's own.

ing with structural considerations. Vintage quilts can be found in abundance, especially old ones that have a hole or tear and are too delicate to be used on the bed. (These tend to be discounted—an added plus!) You can frame the quilt with large salvaged boards, hang it from a piece of pegboard, or place it between two pieces of Plexiglas.

Another great way to cover a large wall space is to pick up a variety of large flower prints or paintings at your local Goodwill. Then paint all the frames the same color and push them together, like a giant collage.

Extra-large artwork, like old movie posters or circus flyers, can also have a big impact with little effort. An old sail, tablecloth, vintage sheet, funky midcentury rug—there are lots of options for bedroom wall art.

This design uses salvaged wood in a variety of ways to create a contemporary space. With its salvaged plywood headboard/shelf, salvaged wood platform bed, and painted dimensional-lumber floor, this room could have a modern look (if painted all black or gray), a cottage look (if painted all white), shabby chic look (if a variety of colors and floral patterns were used), or a Western-Asian fusion look (if the bed frame were left natural with a high-gloss finish and Asian accessories were added). Just a few changes in color, decor, and bedding can radically alter the style. The lights could be vintage chandeliers, retro Atomic-era fixtures, salvaged glass pendants, industry baskets—the list goes on.

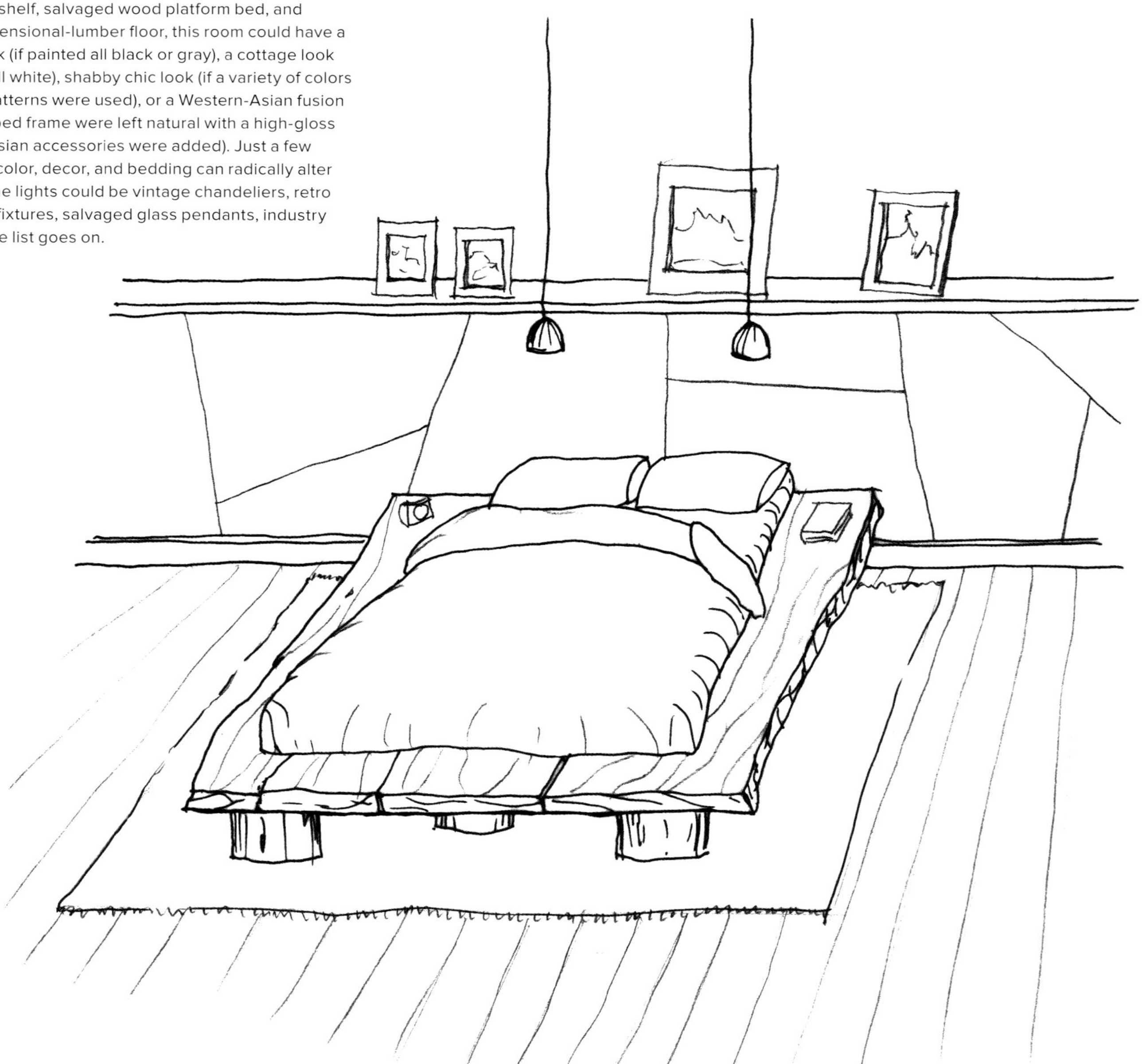

Designed and built by Arciform and the homeowner, Nancy, this recycled shipping container-turned-guesthouse sits only feet from the back door. The walls, ceiling, and swinging bathroom door were made with salvaged felled wood and insulate the old steel box's walls. A vintage French country bed frame sits just steps from a sink made from an old stone bowl and tree trunk. The light above the sink was once an industrial fan and the towel holder is a vintage yard sprinkler. Fun, creative, and cozy, this old shipping box that once traveled the high seas is now landlocked and the perfect spot for an afternoon nap or weekend visit by guests.

Furnishings

Dressers, bureaus, side tables, bed frames, and headboards are the most common pieces you'll find in a bedroom. And second-hand furnishing shops like Goodwill, Habitat for Humanity, Salvation Army, and for-profit consignment shops almost always have a great assortment of bedroom pieces to choose from. You can also find bedroom furniture at garage sales, fairs, and local websites like Craigslist. I've found fantastic vintage and second-hand pieces at church,

Jane Coslick totally changed the look of a second-hand dresser and bed frame by painting them black. With a pop of bright color, this room in her office/guest cottage combines white bedding and walls with black-and-white furnishings and accessories. The salvaged wash table now used as a side table—add just the right touch of warmth to the space.

Cookbook author, designer, and photo stylist Annette Joseph keeps her bedroom soft and romantic with beautiful bedding and a shabby chic side table she found at a garage sale for $20. Annette loved the way it looked, and by keeping it simple she let the patina speak for itself.

school, and senior-center sales—members of these communities bring in their old chairs, beds, bed frames, lamps, quilts, pillows, and more, and all the money goes back into their community. Keep a list of the regular sales near you and check for the dates each year.

One way to update bedroom furnishings is to paint them. Dozens of painting techniques can be used—flat paint with a solid finish, high gloss, distressed, whitewashed, or textured, to name just a few. When you repaint a piece, the right prep work is crucial. If a wooden side table, for example, has a wax or polyurethane finish, that finish needs to be removed for the paint to adhere. A metal piece may need to be heavily sanded or even sandblasted by a professional before it is painted with a metal paint or given a powder coat finish.

◂◂ Designer Teresa Ridon created this bench and it has special significance for her. She and her best friend gathered old barn wood at a ranch in Arizona, from which her friend's husband built the bench. Simply designed and beautifully weathered, this salvaged piece is a perfect ending for the bed. For the mirror beside the bed, Teresa picked up a 7-foot-tall Gothic-style window frame at an antique shop and had it glazed with a mirror finish.

Bed Frames and Headboards

Changing the look of your bedroom can be as easy as changing your bed frame or headboard—whether you repurpose your existing bed or find a second-hand one in your local paper. A new coat of paint on the frame and new slipcover for the headboard (try burlap for a cottage look or silver faux leather for a glam look) will give you an instant, dramatic style. There are also many antique four-poster, canopy, and Craftsman-style beds that can be left as they are, sometimes with only a bit of simple structural work such as tightening some screws or re-gluing a leg. Salvaged wood can be used to create a rustic platform bed with a living edge or a modern clean-lined box with drawers. It's all a matter of taste, style, space, and budget.

When you don't have enough space for a full bed frame, you can create the illusion of a headboard by attaching materials directly to the wall. This allows you to keep a simple metal frame under the bed without the bulk of anything attached to it. Some of the most interesting items I've seen used for headboards are salvaged boards, old doors, wrought-iron gates, shutters, quilts, balusters, and even fabric-covered plywood—all of which can be found at salvage yards and recycle centers.

DESIGN TIP

Before you begin painting your salvaged piece, you must first decide what you want the finished look to be, and then plan your prep work accordingly. A stressed, patina look with layers of paint showing through will require a very different technique than a crisp, clean finish. Choosing the right type of paint is important, too—the choices are abundant, from chalk paints to lacquers, low-sheen to metallic. A paint expert can be a great resource. Visit your local paint store, bring in your piece or a picture of it, and explain what you are trying to do. The professionals there will give you great advice on the steps you should take to get your desired result.

Anna Palmer, owner of Refresh Collections, fills her own master bedroom with retro textiles and furnishings that were found on the Internet and at flea markets and antique shops, where she also seeks products for her online store. The bed skirt is made from vintage ticking fabric and the headboard was slipcovered with similar fabric. Second-hand shops often carry piles of old pillows, handmade blankets, and chairs, upholstered or slipcovered. This bedroom has a cozy 1970s chair, found at a local second-hand shop, tucked in near the bed. Along with the layered blankets and pillows, its vibrant retro color creates the ideal spot for reading with a cup of tea before lights out.The combination of textiles and second-hand furnishings make the room both eclectic and comfortable.

This homeowner fills her own bedroom with antiques and unique finds. The mid-1800s maple four-poster was once three quarters size (like most old beds) but turned it into a queen by disassembling the frame, using what had been the side boards as end boards, and adding new side boards.

Simple in design, this bedroom's midcentury lamp was found at a yard sale and needed no rewiring. Artist and designer Michele de la Vega found the old green filing cabinet at a junk shop and welded the metal legs on herself.

Lighting

Bedroom lighting generally consists of table lamps or wall sconces on either side of the bed. Simple second-hand lamps can be decoupaged and set on the bedside tables, vintage table lamps can be mounted as sconces, or old chandeliers can be hung from the ceiling on either side of the bed. You can even create your own light fixtures from salvaged pulleys and Edison bulbs. Midcentury or antique lamps may need rewiring—an easy job for a professional.

Textiles

Adding salvaged textiles is one of easiest ways to change the look of a bedroom. Tablecloths, bedspreads, sheets, and throws—worn, but still in good condition—are some of the more common types of bedding accessories, but you can also create your own out of old clothing, vintage fabric, or even old cloth sacks, which can be turned into pillowcases. Textiles can be changed out by season, color schemes, or even by a particular period style. When using old fabrics, a good cleaning and airing out are important. Another trick is to place old fabrics in the dryer on high heat (with a dryer sheet) to ensure that there is no insect infestation and to help remove musty smells. Before doing so make sure the material is dry so you don't accidently shrink it.

BATHROOMS

Bathrooms can be our very own private sanctuaries—a place to unwind at the end of the day with a long bath, or your early-morning retreat for a wake-up shower. However you use the space, keep in mind some additional considerations—namely moisture, lighting, and functionality. If the space is well ventilated or especially large, moisture will be less of a problem, but usually it's one of the main design issues. Lighting is also important—do you want dim light for a spa-like environment or brighter task lighting for makeup application or shaving? Finally, there's functionality. Is there a place to hang your towel and store your toiletries? Not having sufficient space for these items can be a daily frustration—one easily avoided with a little advance planning.

Stylist and cookbook author Annette Joseph lives part of the year in Italy and has a great appreciation for its old churches that dot the countryside. Drawing on them for inspiration, she created a bathroom that feels like a sanctuary. The vanity, picked up at an antique shop in historic Marietta, Alabama, was once a prayer stand. The bench opposite it came from the same shop, and the vintage upholstered chair was found in France. The vintage crosses hanging on the wall are part of a collection that Annette has been building for years. The beamed ceiling and large window give the room a calm ethereality.

The bathroom floors in my own home are travertine marble tiles that were seconds from a tile shop. We had a few boxes left over after we'd finished putting in the floors, so we posted them on Craigslist, giving the estimated square footage of what was left. The doors to all the rooms in our home were found at an architectural salvage shop in New Hampshire; we had them stripped and left the natural wood exposed. With old oars and a vintage bottle I picked up at Goodwill for a dollar, our guest bathroom is calming and simple.

Flooring

Floors in bathrooms can range from beautiful salvaged wood to recycled tile to concrete with salvaged aggregate. No matter what the material, however, water issues are a primary concern. If you're using salvaged wood, you need to protect it with the proper coating and make sure your shower, tub, and sink are not leaking water onto the floor. Regular standing water, particularly if there are spaces between the wood pieces, can cause warping. Salvaged wood can also be painted a high-gloss color (or white), which gives a clean look to any bathroom and adds to the water-resistance of the material.

Recycled tile is a popular material for bathroom floors, but not all tile is appropriate for flooring. If you're using tile on the floor, make sure it's non-slip—slate, brick, clay, or honed granite or marble often work well. Many tilers, stone companies, architectural salvage shops, and even rebuild centers will have three or four boxes of these beautiful salvaged tiles left over from other projects—just enough for a small bathroom floor. Online sites are also good places to check.

When it has a significant amount of recycled material in it (like stone, glass, fly ash), concrete is another great salvage option. Long-lasting and durable, concrete is recyclable if you decide you want to replace it with something else. It's also an economical choice, as it functions as the subfloor. As mentioned in Chapter 1, concrete can have countless looks depending on the aggregate that's added to it. Recycled fly ash and crushed glass give

The floors in this Vermont country bathroom are a mix of wide-plank pine and spruce. They were purchased from a local antique dealer who salvaged all the lumber from a 1800s barn. The homeowners sanded and sealed the floor themselves and finished it with three coats of polyurethane. The chair is an English antique and the mirror was a gift from one of the homeowner's grandparents. The pottery is vintage Bennington Pottery, a Vermont company, and the commode (which meant "low cabinet" in the 1700s) is late Victorian. On top of it are a Yellowware jar and porcupine-quill box. Many of these antiques were found at a variety of auctions.

Designed by the homeowners and Arciform, this elegant basement bathroom/laundry room has a concrete floor left in its natural color to look like stone. The lights on either side of the mirror are vintage factory desk lamps purchased from Old Portland Hardware—they add a fun, functional element to the clean white lines of the space. The salvaged sink is from the ReBuild Center.

it the look of stone; glass with a natural dye gives you a bright, colorful look. For a terrazzo floor, the glass or stone can be left in large chunks. Nontoxic dyes and sealers can be used to finish the concrete. And a highly polished look can reflect light. The addition of radiant heat is particularly nice for a bathroom floor.

Walls and Backsplashes

Wall materials—including those in the shower or tub and storage spaces—are a consideration in any bathroom but are particularly important in smaller bathrooms where moisture and humidity are an issue. Both functional and aesthetically versatile, recycled glass tile is a great option because it's nonporous, keeps moisture out, and comes in a variety of shapes and sizes. White subway tiles, sparkly blue tiles that convey a seaside look, circles along the backsplash, one large solid piece used as the counter and backsplash—whatever look you're going for, you can find a tile that will help you achieve it. It's also a product that's widely available, making it easy to keep reusing it.

Salvaged wood—used as wainscoting, beadboard, or even planking—is another great bathroom wall option. You can create a number of looks with salvaged dimensional lumber or even older wide boards. For a nautical look, seal the wood in a boat lacquer, letting the natural color and texture of the wood shine through. For a cottage look, paint the boards white. Half wall,

The laundry area of this bathroom is tucked behind cleverly cut wood from wind-fallen trees. The lines in the wood, routered by Arciform's craftsmen, add another dimension to this already beautiful material. Placing the paneled door on a barn roller helped minimize the need for door swing space while allowing the family to shut the laundry room off from the bathroom with one quick tug.

▲ This just a small sample of the thousands of kinds of recycled glass available at Bedrock Industries in Seattle. Their tile is handmade in their own plant from 100% recycled glass. The color comes from the glass itself—they don't use any pigments. A variety of glass companies around the nation work with recycled glass products.

▶ This bathroom, designed by Michelle de la Vega, has an entire wall built with salvaged wood end-cuts. With a vintage cast-iron tub placed in front of it and a contemporary faucet coming out of the wall, this bathroom has a fresh, eclectic look. The base of the tub was repainted and the claw feet were replaced with more modern salvaged wood stands. Add the old office chair, a light fixture made from recycled parts, and trunk, and you have a very cool space.

▶▶ In the townhouse bathroom of interior designer Teresa Ridlon, a vintage dresser set between two modern sinks serves as storage as well as a place to keep everyday toiletries. A high-gloss white paint helps keep moisture from sinking into the wood. This well-placed salvaged piece gives the bathroom depth and personality, showing that townhouses and condominiums with basic lines can also have texture and style.

full wall—it depends on your space, the amount of salvaged material available to you, and your style preference.

Vanities and Counters

Some of the most gorgeous bathrooms I've seen use unique salvage pieces for the vanity. A vintage dining sideboard, two old wooden trunks stacked together, a farmhouse table, or just one long slab of salvaged wood are all examples of clever styles that can work well as vanities. The major considerations with these items are width (make sure you have enough room for a sink and a faucet, and that the faucet is not too far forward over the bowl) and water tightness. A few good coats of polyurethane or a similar product may be enough to prevent warping, but pieces with edges or cracks need to be sealed with clear caulking or covered with a piece of glass (with a hole for the plumbing).

Of course, salvaged tile or recycled glass counters are also an option, or you can go with something really unique, like a second-hand surfboard placed on a base (with a hole drilled in it for a sink)—perfect for any coastal cottage.

Sinks and Tubs

Keep in mind that sinks can be decorative as well as functional. A recycled glass bowl, sitting on top of a salvaged piece of wood finished with a high-gloss boat stain can look like a piece of art. An extra-large, three-faucet cast-iron sink can be great for a kids' bathroom or a guest bathroom that doesn't need a lot of counter space for daily toiletries. Recycled-metal sinks can be custom-made as well—a drop-in bowl with a recycled concrete countertop lends a more modern feel. Once you decide on a look for your bathroom, you'll find a salvaged or recycled sink to fit it.

Old claw-foot tubs are still very popular, giving instant age and charm, but modern tubs, Jacuzzis, and even drop-ins are also available at rebuild centers. Don't worry if you don't love the color—professionals can reglaze an entire set for you. But don't rush to reglaze those retro pink, blue, and green sinks and tubs—they're coming back into style in full force.

This bathroom off of a kitchen is designed around a huge vintage cast-iron sink from Rejuvenation. The modern recycled-glass tile backsplash looks gorgeous with outlines of foliage and flowers that one of Arciform's craftsmen painted on the walls in lieu of wallpaper. Vintage light fixtures add to the old-fashioned feel of the room and the red stool helps the kids reach the faucets.

DESIGN TIP

Most people don't buy second-hand toilets because older toilets are not low-flow. But that doesn't mean you should send your old toilet to the dump. There are many companies, including the California company Fire Clay, who clean them, smash them up, and make gorgeous tile out of the pulverized ceramic. Fire Clay's "Debris Series" tile has over 60% recycled material and is available in 112 colors.

Fixtures and Hardware

Faucets, handles, drawer pulls, showerheads and rods, towel racks, robe hooks—these are just a few of the ordinary items you find in bathrooms, but they don't have to *look* ordinary. Old plumbing handles can be turned into drawer pulls; salvaged copper piping can be used for towel racks and toilet-paper holders. These types of

The countertop in this entryway bathroom was made from wood salvaged from land that was cleared when the house was built. Preserving the wood's character, the homeowner cut it in a curved shape, allowing room for a modern toilet and small metal washbasin. Using the same wood, she created a backsplash that gives the counter a more substantial presence.

Annette Joseph—whose church-inspired bathroom was pictured earlier (see p. 75)—loves to travel. When she spied this antique wash sink, with backsplash textured by old insect marks, on a trip to Belgium, she knew it would be perfect for her guest bathroom. Displayed next to the sink are pieces from her collection of vintage linens (with some new ones mixed in). With the inside shutter window, this bathroom has an Old World European feel.

Artisan and designer Colleen Frederick used a silver leaf distressed with black oil paint to cover her vintage claw-foot tub and the drawer faces and panels on the second-hand dresser she uses as a vanity. The backsplash was made from salvaged tile left over from a project her husband's company, Deco Stone and Tile, did. The wall sconces, which they rewired, are antiques that Colleen found at Star's Antique Mall. She picked up the mirror second-hand. With bright blue walls and red curtains, the bathroom is both dramatic and cheery.

This eclectic bathroom schematic was designed solely around salvaged material. The mirrors are a collection of second-hand finds, easy to pick up at your local Goodwill, Habitat for Humanity, or Salvation Army. The countertop is reclaimed antique wood (wide and thick) supported by vintage metal brackets. Recycled sinks sit right on top. The beadboard is made from recycled dimensional lumber (easy to paint white and cut to paneling size), and the lights are common industrial pendants that can be found online or made at a custom salvage lighting shop. Piecing together a salvage design can be like creating a piece of artwork, layering the colors and textures together.

recycled plumbing fixtures, both modern and vintage, can be found at architectural salvage shops, rebuild centers, and online. Modern plumbing can look great with salvaged wood; vintage plumbing can look great with modern concrete counters, backsplashes, and shower walls. Single-stem faucets from the mid-1970s may seem boring, but put three of them next to one another along a trough-style sink and your guests will say “wow!” when they enter the bathroom. Peruse the plumbing fixtures and hardware at your local rebuild and salvage shops and see what you find. Some items are so unique that you could design an entire room around them.

DESIGN TIP

Salvaged metal comes in all shapes and forms and can be used with any bathroom style. Items like recycled metal restaurant tables, drop-in sinks, and vintage claw-foot tubs can be purchased and installed as-is. Recycled aluminum can be melted down and used to custom-make a hammered sink that would look spectacular set in a beautiful piece of reclaimed wood. Or you can buy metal sheeting and cut it to fit a countertop or wrap it around a salvaged plywood base. Copper is a great metal and can be up to 85% recycled. Add a sealant to retain the shiny look or let it patina into a beautiful green.

▸ Designed by the homeowner and Arciform, this bathroom in a recycled shipping container is small in space but big on design. The shower is a galvanized-steel feeding trough from a farm store. The walls were made from wood salvaged from fallen trees on the property of Arciform owners Anne and Richard De Wolf. (The lines in the wood were cut in for effect.) The steel strapping on the door creates instant storage.

◂◂ The guest bathroom in Jane Coslick's island cottage has a clean yet festive feel with a polka-dot bathmat hanging over the salvaged claw-foot tub. She added shells to an old mirror, and the windows on the salvaged door were updated with privacy glass.

DESIGN TIP

Design teams, architects, and homeowners deservedly get a lot of credit when it comes to salvage design. But we shouldn't forget about all the builders who work with the materials. They are the ones in the trenches figuring out how to incorporate one-of-a-kind salvaged pieces into a new building design or a remodel (which can be even more difficult at times). So when the sawdust is flying and the measuring tapes are zipping, we need to show our appreciation for their hard work in making our salvage dreams come true. Without their enthusiasm and support, many salvage design ideas would never make it past the drawing board.

▲ Homeowner Dana Murphy repurposed these old plumbing handles herself. She picked them up at an antique shop and filled the backs with epoxy. Then she drilled in screws to create handles for her bathroom cabinets. The recycled glass tile in the tub surround adds a bright pop of color. The exposed red-oak beams, salvaged from an old house two states away, highlight the post-and-beam style of the home and add a nice texture and layer of design.

▸ Once filled with a glass or wood panel, this door now doubles as a full-length mirror—a brilliant alternative to hanging a mirror on the back of a door. You could do the same for bedroom, closet, or pantry doors.

In this contemporary penthouse apartment in New York City, the bathroom sink was simply placed on top of a piece of salvaged wood that serves as the countertop. The same wood was used throughout the apartment, including as wall paneling in the kitchen and entrance area. Besides the patterned tile floor, the vintage stools are the only decoration in this attractive, clean-lined space.

Shelving and Storage

Salvaged shelving and storage can be as simple as vintage hooks on an old piece of wood, a metal luggage rack, and a second-hand dresser or cupboard. Apple crates hung on their sides are great for storing towels—cover an entire wall with them for a big design statement. An antique bedspread hung on a spring rod will not only hide plastic containers stored behind it, but also give the bathroom a fun pop of color and texture.

DESIGN TIP

French doors, tall glass cabinet doors, and cabinet doors with wood panels that can be easily punched out are in abundance at architectural salvage shops and rebuild centers. You can even use storm doors and nine-paned windows turned sideways as doors for medicine cabinets, linen closets, pantries, or cupboards. To hide your toiletries, use frosted glass, metal mesh, or even recycled chicken wire backed by burlap for a shabby chic look. Replacing the panels with mirrors not only makes the piece functional but also adds light and depth to the room.

The shelf above the toilet is an old railroad luggage rack and the tiny vintage dresser next to the toilet is a perfect place to store toilet paper. Tiny salvage touches like these add tons of character to this simple yet elegant bathroom.

These custom-made medicine-cabinet doors are a great example of what you can do with paneled cabinetry. Pop out the wood panel in the middle and add decorative metal mesh or glass panels. The vintage blue glass knobs on these doors are a nice additional touch.

Designer Stephanie Larrowe handpicks vintage textiles for the handbags and furniture her company, TOTeM, makes, and she did the same for her own richly vibrant living room. The Spanish adobe-style Los Angeles home is filled with unique second-hand furniture pieces that her team reupholstered in old Mexican blankets and vintage embroidered pieces found at flea markets and antique fairs. The coffee table is a piece of framed artwork laid on top of two vintage Chinese garden pieces. Vintage wall sconces with red shades flank the curved windows that show off the colorful California flora. The bold and beautiful palette of this room reminds us that we can think beyond beige when designing our living spaces.

Living Rooms & Dens

Living rooms differ from other rooms in that they are meant to be gathering places. Whether it's a fireplace, coffee table, or bank of floor-to-ceiling windows showing off a spectacular view, every living room should have a spot that pulls the room together. Its size, its relationship to other spaces, and the placement of windows all come into play when designing this area.

▸▸ Combining bright colors with neutrals and incorporating various salvaged materials, artist and designer Colleen Frederick created a comfortable, eclectic living room. Her husband, a tiler, picked up tiles left over from a job to create the fireplace surround. The mantel was made from discarded moulding from a steel factory, and the glass doors are from a salvage yard. Colleen transformed the chairs, which were once in a dentist's office, by painting them in a distressed silver leaf and reupholstering them in wool from second-hand men's suits. The rewired vintage ceiling fixture they brought with them from their old home. The vintage copper bucket that holds the wood is just one of the many decor details that Colleen found at a variety of second-hand and salvage shops in town. She found the coffee table legs in a free pile and had the tabletop made out of SlateScape (recycled paper and cement). The artwork is Colleen's own.

DESIGN TIP

Looking to stock your own bookshelves? Try online sites for second-hand books, specialty second-hand bookstores, or your local library's annual book sale. Libraries often offer even deeper discounts on the last day of the sale, sometimes selling hardcover books for as little as fifty cents. It's a win-win—a great local cause, and lots of books!

Flooring and Walls

The options for living room flooring are essentially the same as those for kitchens, dining rooms, bedrooms, and bathrooms (refer to Chapters 1 and 2 for more information on types of flooring). Salvaged hardwood, reclaimed heart of pine, recycled Mexican tile, concrete with salvaged aggregate—the choice depends on the overall look you want to achieve. Are you going for a dark, elegant, formal look in your high-ceilinged 19th-century townhouse? Ebony stained salvaged oak flooring might be a perfect choice. Designing a funky, open artist's loft? Try using salvaged pieces of plywood arranged in a jigsaw pattern, adhered right to the concrete and painting the floor in a fun Op Art–type pattern. (My first book, *Salvage Secrets*, shows how do to this.)

Chapters 1 and 2 also detail wall-covering options. Paneled gray wood is great for a rustic cabin feel. If you're looking for a more traditional look, cut some vintage doors in half, place them along the bottom half of the wall, add a piece of trim along the top as a chair rail, and you have added beautiful wainscoting to your room, not to mention character, texture, and depth. Or, consider walls of salvaged-wood bookcases or walls covered in vintage fabric—the choice is all yours.

Before making your flooring and wall decisions, however, it's a good idea to consider the rest of the space—especially the spot in the room that's going to be the focal point. Will the paneling you're thinking about for the walls distract from the view out the windows? Will the terrazzo concrete that looked great in a magazine be too busy next to the brick fireplace that's central to your design? Whatever the focal point of your living room is, you want the rest of the design to highlight—not compete—with it.

Fireplaces and Hearths

Building a fireplace or resurfacing an old one gives you many opportunities to use salvaged or recycled material, whether it's tile, stone, brick, or metal. Recycled porcelain tile, like Fireclay's "Debris Series," is available in solid colors as well as in decorative Mexican, Moroccan, and Italian patterns, and you can easily get these pieces cut to size to fit your fireplace design. You can also combine materials by setting a tile mural or border in a brick, marble, slate, or

28
GENESIS
DEGAS
Beautiful

This 1970s brick fireplace was resurfaced with a tinted concrete mixture, totally changing the look of the room. The mantel is a piece of antique Chinese wood. Modern-style furnishings and some funky retro pieces, including the vintage bowling table, retro light fixture, and glass table, give this space a sleek, mod look.

Homeowners Dana and Raymond Murphy designed their Vermont post-and-beam home around certain features, including this 1700s Rumford fireplace and stone hearth salvaged from a house that was being torn down in Connecticut. Many of the red oak beams are from the same house. This is an excellent example of historic salvage restoration.

You can add "wow" to any wall with three simple salvaged materials. Flip a hollow-core door on its side and attach it to a barn slider to hide a television. You can enhance the door with black paint and a decoupaged collage of black-and-white family photos. Line the bottom of the wall with recycled kitchen cabinets (also painted black)—remove the doors and slide in some old baskets for easy storage. Add some stacked apple crates (painted black) on top of the cabinet next to the television and you've got a simple entertainment area in your living space.

granite fireplace. Another tile option is recycled glass. Glass mosaics (variations of all white, all gray, or even deep red) work well with fireplaces or gas inserts that have a more modern, sleek design. A whole wall can be covered in the recycled tile, with just the black gas inset box standing out.

Salvaged metal is another option. It's often used in tiles and sheets, such as hammered copper or galvanized aluminum with a rustic patina. And then there are the old standbys of salvaged brick or stone, including marble or granite pieces. Architectural salvage shops collect old pieces of marble mantels, surrounds, counters, and more. These pieces of stone can be cut to size for your needs. Also check out stone companies, many of which sell salvaged and left-over stone, and brick companies, which often sell vintage bricks they have recovered from decommissioned buildings.

Of course, aesthetics are important to consider when choosing fireplace and mantel materials, but

▸▸ Following the tradition of many cottages throughout the islands off the coast of Georgia, designer Jane Coslick used a clean white palette with pops of color for her own living room. Second-hand furnishings were slipcovered in white fabric. An old beadboard trunk, also painted white, helps with storage in this small cottage by the ocean. The vintage dresser mirror and barstool were painted turquoise.

DESIGN TIP

Furniture is one of the least-recycled items in a household. According to a 2009 U.S. EPA report, it accounted for 9.8 million tons (over 4%) of household waste. We can begin to change those numbers by repurposing or recovering our own furnishings, sharing them with others on sites like Craigslist or Freecycle, donating them to recycle centers, or selling them at garage or estate sales.

functionality is critical, too. Bricks, stones, and tiles have varying degrees of heat resistance and structural stability. Consult with a stone company or mason before purchasing your material. He or she will be able to tell you whether the material you're considering is sufficiently heat-resistant for your particular project.

Furnishings

The living room gets the most attention when it comes to moveable furniture. Couches, chairs, coffee tables, side tables, floor lamps, table lamps, and rugs are the main pieces that make this room a *living* room.

Old upholstered furnishings can be used as-is, or they can be reupholstered or slipcovered. When you find an old piece of furniture that fits your size and shape needs, check its structural integrity to make sure it's worth slipcovering or upholstering. Cushions can always be replaced but frames are tougher to fix. The frame should be made of real wood (not pressed board) and should be structurally sound, with dovetail joints or dowels or screws—not staples. And don't buy it if you can feel the frame under the padding.

Repurposing material to create your own furnishings—salvaged-wood coffee tables, pallets used as couches, end tables made from industrial machinery—guarantees that you'll have a one-of-a-kind piece. If you spend enough time on the Internet or looking through design books, you'll see just how creative you can get with repurposed materials. And don't forget to look to local artisans to help you think outside the box, too—one I know of, Aaron Stein, makes chairs out of old car seats and salvaged license plates.

As I mentioned in Chapter 1, however, you need to make sure that the chair you just found at a garage sale isn't a collectible before you reupholster it or take it apart. If you've ever seen *Antiques Roadshow*, you know that it could end up being as valuable as a Babe Ruth baseball card—or worth only the $5 you paid for it. Figuring out whether the piece is a collectible may take some time, research, and, in most cases, an expert in the field. The four main criteria used by experts are rarity, provenance (origin), quality, and condition. Color, patina, and popular styles come into play as well. If you suspect your piece may be worth something but you can't find a signature or stamp on it, take some

BY THE SEA

SIBLEY BIRDS
World Cruising
ROUTES

Every single decorative touch in designer Teresa Ridlon's stylish townhouse is salvaged. The mantel is vintage (repainted) along with everything on it. Salvaged metal crates—old bottle carries—are used as a side table, an oversized French vintage wicker basket serves as the coffee table, and old shutters from Belgium (but purchased in Phoenix) are used instead of curtains—and the list goes on. Throughout the space Teresa created small vignettes of salvaged and vintage finds, creating three separate areas in one living room.

◀◀ A collection of salvaged, second-hand, and found items in neutral colors gives my living room a warm, calming feel. I found the white chair at a recycle center and re-covered it with a painter's tarp. The coffee table was made by Champlain Valley Antiques out of salvaged wood. The side table is made of salvaged wood and metal; the lamp on it was one I found at Goodwill and decoupaged with dictionary pages. The fireplace hearth was created out of three pieces of leftover soapstone from a kitchen project. All the accessories were found at antique and second-hand shops.

Artist and designer Michelle de la Vega went for a midcentury feel in this living room space. The vintage Japanese wall art was being thrown away by a shop down the street from her welding studio. She made the metal couch, repurposed filing-cabinet side table, and table in front of the couch herself. Then she added some recycled finds, including the old office chair, vintage lamp, and magazine holder.

pictures to your local expert or call a qualified appraiser to come by and look at it. If you live near an auction house, call to see whether they offer appraisals (some even have special days when you can bring in your piece for a free evaluation). You never know—you may have a piece worth collecting, not covering.

Pulling It All Together

Once you've gotten the basics of your space down, it's time think about accessories. How do you want the room to look? Country? Modern? Retro? Or would you prefer an eclectic look, filling it with things you love no matter the style? This approach has become more and more popular as homeowners move toward design and decor that allows them to live comfortably in their spaces.

The display of your salvaged pieces is just as important as the pieces themselves. As I did research for this book, I discovered some basic themes that homeowners and designers seemed to return to when pulling together salvaged elements for their designs.

CONTRASTING FEATURES

It's fun to peek inside a cold, industrial shipping container used as a guest cottage and see warm reclaimed-wood walls and soft vintage bedding—a surprising contrast to the metal exterior. Mixing too many strong design statements together can create a distracting mishmash, but sometimes two bold features

◂ These unique metal tables, made from hoods of scrapped cars and trucks, are the brainchild of Joel Hester, the owner of the Weld House and an artisan who makes a variety of furnishings out of old cars. With their original patina, every one of his pieces is different. Joel is one of thousands of artisans and small business owners who make amazing pieces out of material once headed to overburdened landfills or scrap piles.

▾ Decorating a living room wall can be as simple as layering old frames like I did here. These beautiful old frames have a great deal of texture and speak for themselves. I used a central frame with a print for this piece, but often that's not even necessary. See the Do-It-Yourself chapter for step-by-step directions on creating your own layered-frame decor.

will perfectly complement each other. Whether you're contrasting warm with cold, ornamented with a more clean-lined piece, or a pattern with a solid—balance is key.

COLOR SCHEMES

A critical part of the design scheme, color goes a long way toward establishing the mood of your space. A living room in soothing blues and neutrals will feel very different from one in dramatic red and black. There are a few different approaches to color schemes in design. One is to go monochrome—all blues for a cottage home, for example, or different shades of white for a glamorous apartment. Another is to offset one color with bursts of another color (or couple of colors). A vintage pink metal cabinet against a white wall or a bright yellow chandelier in a gray-toned midcentury room will give the space a surprising pop of color. In some cases, mixing a bunch of colors together is the best way to go, creating a bright and happy visual flurry (see p. 92).

Bright red and floral-patterned pillows look great on these second-hand matching chairs that have been slipcovered with cotton painter's tarps. The couch has been covered in two white bedspreads found at a garage sale for $5 each. The coffee table is custom-made from salvage wood and the lamp, side table, and metal basket are all second-hand finds at the local Goodwill store. Together, these pieces create a welcoming, eclectic style that is very popular today.

REPETITION

Annette Joseph's church-inspired bathroom (see p. 75), with her collection of crosses on the wall, is a great example of repetition as a design strategy. Whether it's bell jars, vintage postcards of waterfalls, old glass power line insulators, embroidered handkerchiefs, or metal cogs from industrial machinery, there is power in numbers.

Repetition can be achieved through structural elements as well—think of the vaulting in all those gorgeous European cathedrals, or the wide arching doorways in New York's Grand Central Station.

LAYERS UPON LAYERS

Layering similar textures, colors, and styles will give your living room warmth, richness, and depth. Start with whitewashed reclaimed-wood beadboard walls, add an antique table, an old wool runner, and then some vintage vases. If you're more of a minimalist, try layering just a few pieces of decor—a second-hand patterned throw over a vintage velveteen chair, or several Oriental carpets overlaying one another.

FOCAL POINTS

An extra-large vintage chandelier, an old movie poster that covers the entire wall, or a big piece of old machinery with a glass tabletop—these kinds of focal points will capture anyone's attention in a room. Updating an old fireplace with recycled glass and vintage tiles (with Moroccan- or Mexican-style patterns) will provide a dramatic color focal point to your living room. Think about what you want to highlight and what kind of salvaged material or piece can help you to do it.

WABI SABI

Wabi sabi (the love of imperfection) seems to be inherent in all designs that include salvaged and recycled material and pieces. It's almost impossible not to embrace the imperfections of a material, whether that imperfection is naturally occurring (as it is in wood) or comes through years of use (as with an old desk, couch, or chair). Sometimes designers intentionally include imperfections in their materials—at times even highlighting them. Other times the imperfections are more subtle, giving the piece character and substance.

PATINA IN ALL ITS FORMS

Color that comes naturally with age—the weathered gray of old wood, the blue-greens of oxidized copper, the iridescence of tarnished silver, the rich russets of rusty metal—can be accentuated in design instead of hidden. These patinas are not only beautiful but also reflect the history of the material, hinting at its use before it arrived in your home.

This shabby chic living room proves that a condominium can have great style. Attaching shelves to an old salvaged door and then adding a light and daybed to it, designer and homeowner Renee Tornabene was able to create a relaxing corner filled with character. The old suitcases, found at vintage shops around Phoenix, serve as a side table to the couch. The columns on either side of the gas fireplace add another layer of design to a once-simple structure.

◀◀ This entryway has an Old World feel with its antique Swedish bench, picked up in the south of France by homeowner, Annette Joseph. Annette found the two vintage bottles on the right in Italy, and the green ceramic one at the store Europe 2 You. The floor's antique tile pavers are from a monastery in France.

Entryways & Outdoor Living

ENTRYWAYS

The entryway is the first place people see in your home, but it also often serves as the mudroom. So how do you make it efficient for storage as well as attractive for first impressions? By combining salvaged materials, you can create a space that works for your needs. Storage for coats, hats, mittens, and boots can be made from salvaged goods like old crates, as can benches for sitting while you put on your shoes. And there's no reason these functional pieces can't also be prominent design features that contribute to the aesthetic of your home.

▸ The ReSource Store in Burlington, Vermont, is just one of the many nonprofit rebuild and recycle centers around the nation that collect leftover tile supplies from homeowners and builders. Piles of mismatched ceramic, porcelain, and clay tiles await a new home. You can easily mix and match them to create patterns if there isn't enough of one kind for your whole floor. If you're looking for more decorative pieces but can't seem to find enough in one spot, try specialty stores and online sites that make new decorative patterned tiles out of recycled material.

▸▸ The entryway tile was found in the seconds pile at a tile shop. The sideboard is a vintage Stickley piece, the mirror was made using salvaged wood trim, and the Goodwill lamp was decoupaged with paper bags. The iron gate was found at an antique shop.

Flooring

The floors of an entryway see a lot of wear and tear, so it's important to choose materials that hold up well. Salvaged tile makes cleanup a breeze, but reclaimed wood with a lot of texture is also a smart choice because it hides dirt and muddy footprints until you have a chance to clean them up. Salvaged metal grates are also a handy addition to a mudroom entryway—you can insert them into the floor and use them to stamp out your boots and shoes.

Salvaged brick in a herringbone pattern is great for a small space, but it needs to be sealed because it's a porous material. If your entryway is small, you may be able to find scraps of stone slabs that can be cut to fit the space. Concrete with salvaged aggregate is also a popular flooring material for entryways—an area rug can be used to add warmth and texture. Area and throw rugs can be found at a variety of salvage and second-hand shops, or you can paint a new scrap carpet piece in a pattern of your choosing (see p. 253). Once you've decided which salvage material works best for your floor, you can proceed with the rest of the design.

DESIGN TIP

When you learn about the quality of the reclaimed wood you are considering, you get a better idea of where and how to use it. Some pieces are great for flooring but too thin for an island top; others might be great for wall planking or even a cupboard but are not structurally sound enough for an exposed beam running through the kitchen. Wood experts, salvage shop owners, and other professionals can help you navigate the woodpile.

live
love
laugh

DESIGN TIP

Paneling can be created with a variety of types of dimensional lumber. You can have wide paneling with salvaged plywood and trim, make beadboard from salvaged flat trim pieces, or create horizontal paneling from old floorboards or even 1x6s. Layering salvaged lumber and trim provides a pleasing visual variety.

The ceiling in this entryway is made of old cabinet doors painted white to give a unique paneled look. For visual fun, various salvaged knobs were added to the door panels in the ceiling. The light fixture is a rewired antique with its glass globes removed. The wall sconce and framed-in stained glass are also vintage pieces. The eclectic coat hangers in different shapes and sizes are from Aurora Mills Architectural Salvage Shop. "True" divided light windows—meaning the wood trim pieces that divide the window are part of the structure, not simply inserted on top of the glass—on both sides of the room were salvaged from the ReBuilding Center in Portland. Any of these accents could have easily been thrown into a dumpster because they didn't match anything else, but here they come together to create a beautiful, welcoming space.

By using moveable pieces, including an old army trunk, a second-hand table, and reclaimed crates, the owner of this condominium was able to create an attractive entrance space without involving any structural elements. The second-hand mirrors, whose frames she painted white, bounce light into the darker space.

A used-office-supply store has tons of affordable, second-hand shelving available for instant storage in any entryway. Give a chic industrial look to any loft, apartment, or home by lining a wall with these shelves and using them to hold a variety of salvaged storage baskets and boxes. Add some pizzazz with identical bright baskets in a Moroccan fabric pattern or another attention-grabbing color. You can even apply a metal paint to the racks, changing them from office gray to hot blue or winter white.

Wall Units and Storage

Instant storage can be created in lots of ways using salvaged material—cover an entire wall with salvaged beadboard, trim pieces with hooks, or old wooden apple crates; use blanket boxes as seats and storage; install old pine cupboards, school lockers, or metal office shelving. Determine what seems to collect in your entryway—skis, rackets, and other sports equipment, boots, hats, beach towels, jackets—and decide on your salvaged storage units accordingly. Also think about whether you want these items hidden or in plain sight. Beach towels might look great hanging from an open rack, whereas coats and snowsuits might best be stored behind a couple of salvaged closet doors.

This entryway design combines recycled decorative tiling with office shelving, salvaged baskets, a second-hand window transom, and built-in closets with old office doors studded with pebbled glass. The space seems straight out of a 1950s spy movie (especially if you add black letters to the glass) while being able to hold lots of coats, jackets, and boots. Transform the vibe entirely by simply changing the colors—use solid-color tiles, paint the cabinets and doors a bright blue—and you've instantly got a "coastal"—style mudroom.

▲ This salvaged-wood bench runs along the edge of the kitchen. With a built-in dog bed, drawers for phones and keys, and a sitting area, the space is cozy as well as functional. Hung beneath the beautiful salvaged red-oak beams, wall sconces custom made from champagne glasses make the spot pleasant for a quiet read when you're not getting ready to head outside.

▶ These old lockers, at Sweet Salvage in Phoenix, would be perfect for a busy family's entryway storage, especially if they flanked a salvaged bench with a hook rack above it. Each family member could have his or her very own locker for books, bags, phones, and keys.

DESIGN TIP

Don't forget to check out your local stone supplier's remnant piles for left-over pieces of slate, bricks, and more. These types of salvaged stone are great for patios and entranceways. The materials in remnant piles are often greatly discounted, too. Other places to look are Craigslist, Freecycle, Front Porch Forum, and your local newspaper, where homeowners often post listings for leftover materials from building or remodel projects.

Unique paneling with old doors and mismatched salvaged hooks give a quirky elegance to this mudroom, designed by Arciform Design Build, a company that loves working with salvaged materials in innovative ways. Mismatched hooks and knobs are easy to find at architectural salvage shops.

One of the rooms I worked on for the DIY NETWORK video series, this entrance porch was once used for storage but now is an enjoyable breakfast nook. I found the once rusty wrought-iron patio set at an antique shop and then sanded and painted it in a warm, coffee-with-cream color. A simple bench, painted to match the wall, holds several antiques the homeowner found in a closet. The light fixture was a $5 find at a rebuild center—a coat of blue paint on the metal to get rid of the brassy look was all it needed.

OUTDOOR LIVING

More and more homeowners are designing outdoor living spaces, and not surprisingly, some of the most popular additions are porches (screened in or open), patios, and covered decks. A comfortable outdoor area that flows seamlessly from the interior will extend your living space during warm months.

Your geographic location will be a major factor in the design and decor of your outdoor living space. Warm climates allow for more flexibility, of course, but patios and porches in more northern areas can become favorite spots during the summer—or even during the cooler seasons if you have an outdoor fireplace or other heating element. And salvaged finds, of course, can help turn your outdoor space into a much-loved retreat.

This outdoor patio in the Phoenix area is used a lot. With a variety of unique finds at garage sales, like the birdcage, old bench, and tricycle, the homeowner was able to create an outdoor refuge filled with plants and flowers.

▲ This outdoor space in Portland, shown in both photos above, is the perfect place to enjoy a glass of iced tea or evening cocktail. Kerri Hoyt-Pack, the homeowner, found the green table at Stars Antique Mall—she fills the deep drawers with ice for serving drinks. The white metal couch, chairs, and table were picked at another local antique shop. Layered with vintage and salvaged pillows and linens, this outdoor living room can be enjoyed throughout the seasons.

▶▶ A stunning front porch greets visitors at designer Jane Coslick's seaside cottage office. The second-hand wicker chairs and metal couch are all different in style, but Jane pulled them together by upholstering them in the same striped fabric with matching striped pillows. The zebra rug makes the space feel more like a room than a porch—a great place to start the day with a hot cup of coffee.

DESIGN TIP

Start collecting! Even before you begin construction, you can start collecting items you know you will want in your home—a farmhouse table for the kitchen, perhaps, or salvaged tiles for the backsplash. Whether it's high-end appliances, vintage cabinetry, or a few boxes of leftover tile, the best stuff does not last long in salvage shops and rebuild centers, so you have to get it while you can. Plus, it may take a while to find the perfect combination of salvage materials for your space, so it's best to get a head start. Don't forget to check online sites, but try to stay as local as possible for ease of transport and questions about construction and material.

Revolver, a small chain of salons in New York City, has a unique approach to their styling stations. The countertop is built with vintage speakers that work. Stenciling was added to the mirrors, and a huge chandelier made from old blow dryers that have been painted gold hangs near the front door (you can see it reflected in the mirror). Revolver is just one of thousands of small businesses across the nation that give themselves a unique look and brand through the use of salvaged material.

Retail Inspiration

Big or small, many of today's businesses—offices, retail shops, restaurants, even the hospitality industry—are brand-building by selling their products in a unique way, and salvage designs and displays play a key role in helping them showcase their individuality. These spaces ignite creativity not only in their employees and management but also in homeowners, who, if they're paying careful attention, can take the design ideas back home with them.

I've seen an Urban Outfitters store with hundreds of salvaged glass vases entwined with strands of light and hung from the ceiling, creating a one-of-a-kind light fixture; a lobby

Industrie Denim's changing rooms are a study in layering. The walls are first covered in old maps, pages of design catalogues, and wallpaper samples. Then, layered on top of that is an old mirror or door with old mirror. Each dressing room floor is unique, with salvaged tiles from the reclaim center. Mismatched doors purchased at a salvage yard were painted in different colors, with a crackle texture. Above the dressing rooms are vintage industrial lights and old photographs. Together, these salvage-friendly design elements make trying on a pair of designer jeans more than just a simple shopping trip—it becomes an experience.

wall at The Postcard Inn, in Florida, covered in vintage and recycled beach postcards; Anthropologie storefront displays filled with creative salvage treatments; and a restaurant in The Standard, a boutique hotel in New York City, whose floor is made entirely from pennies.

When you're a customer, these types of salvage touches can really stand out. How can they convert to your home? Easy. You may choose to use different, more functional materials, but the shape, size, or placement of the design can be applied to your home with little fuss. You'll get plenty of ideas for your home—and even your own business—as you go through this chapter.

At a grocery store, we never look twice at the old metal baskets that hold the veggies and fruits, but here they become an attractive display for jeans. Thankfully, a grocery store recycled these baskets instead of throwing them away, and they were subsequently bought at auction by Rudophe Faulcon. This kind of vintage industrial vibe appears throughout Industrie Denim in small vignettes—an old door displays jeans, vintage farm tables hold T-shirts. You can use retail design as an inspiration for your own home projects. The metal grocery display would be great in an entryway for hats and mittens, or in a bathroom for an array of toiletries.

Old factory machinery parts are usually discarded because it's almost impossible to find a use for them. But we're seeing more and more of these bulky metal pieces being reused as displays, bases for tables, and more. Solid and strong, they remind us of our nation's industrial era. The railing here was also made from old metal scraps welded together.

INDUSTRIE DENIM

San Francisco, California
Scottsdale, Arizona
www.industriedenim.com

Industrie Denim's mission is to be the best denim store in the world. A San Francisco–based retail brand from the folks behind Levi's and American Rag, the store carries many earth-conscious and eco-friendly denim and other products. Only recently opened, the space is a salvage lover's paradise. It was designed by architect Michael Robinson and interior designer Rudolphe Faulcon, who scoured the area for the most unique architectural salvage items around and incorporated their finds not only into the design but also into the

DESIGN TIP

These businesses show us that designing with reclaimed material can be chic, beautiful, and sustainable—not to mention, very unique! These are just a handful of the thousands of retailers, offices, and hospitality-industry businesses using recycled and salvaged material. Remember, they also use local builders, architects, designers, and artisans, who can be a great resource for you as well.

Mix and match pieces of Moroccan tile, and add a vintage leather chair and an old piano, painted orange, with its legs removed, and you instantly have a mod, industrial, hip aesthetic. But the salvage doesn't stop there. Recycled trumpets have been flattened and hung on the wall, the metal railing is recycled, and the lighting is vintage. Even the handbag hanging on the standing display is made from recycled scarves. Pick one or all of these elements and transfer them to your home. A smaller piano could serve as a coffee table. The stairs are one of my favorite design elements—the mismatched tiles give vibrancy to the space. Recycled tile can be found in abundance at rebuild centers, but not always in large quantities, making the mix-and-match strategy a great one.

Salvaged pieces are used here for both their visual effect and functional capability. Old tables display merchandise, and the rough-hewn, reclaimed red barn wood on the wall is a nice visual separator for the brands. The well-placed vintage light breaks up the standard store-display lighting. The lockers hold smaller items and give height to the standing displays. The balance between artful displays and high-end merchandise makes this a fun store to explore. Translation to your home? Easy. The red barn wood is gorgeous—it would make a great headboard in your bedroom, with two of these amazing vintage lights hanging down from the ceiling above the side tables.

When I spotted these old Murano light fixtures that once were gaslights, I was thrilled to see they had been converted to electrical and reused. It's hard to convince people not to be afraid of older lighting. There are hundreds of companies and professionals who will convert or repair old lighting for you, as these designers have done here. Rudolphe Faulcon found these big-statement pieces at auction. Combined with the salvaged benches, stools, doors, and industrial worktables, they add to the store's cornucopia of salvage design ideas. And don't overlook the film negatives hung on the concrete wall. You can do something similar. Do you have blocks from your childhood? Perhaps they can be made into a wall decoration. Old stamps, buttons, or letters? They might work in your kitchen, dining, or living room. One small recycled piece might not be enough to work with, but 10, 15, or even 50 can become a creative art display.

The Bancroft's unpretentious rooms are filled with recycled and repurposed goods, some even from the old rooms themselves. What used to be armoires in the room were remade into desks and the repurposing took place on the property. The headboards, once painted green, were refinished. The curtains are made from recycled polyester and soda bottles, and the lamps, once an orange color with an Oriental pattern, were painted over with a metallic paint. The vintage chair and second-hand books were added to the room as well. The framed pieces in each room have a theme—in this room it's the Department of Ophthalmology at UC Berkeley, with vintage papers and drawings, found in old desks in the department.

function of the store. With its funky, industrial edge, this design proves that you can be inspired by the past while embracing modern technology.

THE BANCROFT HOTEL

Berkeley, California
www.bancrofthotel.com

The Bancroft Hotel is a charming bed and breakfast located on the edge of the University of California's Berkeley campus. A National Historic Landmark building that was recently renovated, the boutique hotel has 22 quaint rooms. This hotel is a shining example of how to repurpose and recycle in a renovation. The owner, Daryl Ross, made a commitment to green renovation and assembled a consulting and design team that included David Gottfried, the founder of the U.S. and World Green Building Council, Dan Smith, a green architect based in Berkeley, and principal green designer Kelly LaPlante. This team not only preserved the history of the hotel but also made it environmentally friendly in every way, from the building practices and materials used (and reused) to the installation of energy-efficient fixtures and appliances. Their goal was to inspire guests and help them see the beauty and durability of the environmentally friendly materials that make up their rooms, lobby, and other community areas.

▲ The interesting retro-pattern tile on the lobby floor of the Bancroft Hotel is from Fireclay Tile, a California-based company that creates ceramic and glass products using sustainable manufacturing process and recycled materials. This tile is from their Runway Collection line, by interior designer Kelly LaPlante. It's made from recycled toilets (sanitized and crushed in a huge pit). Ceramic tiles come in hundreds of different styles and colors and can make a great addition to your entryway or bathroom floor (if they're made from recycled toilets, like these are, they're also not a bad conversation piece!). The second-hand chair is recovered with a fabric made from recycled polyester and soda bottles.

In the breakfast room is a vintage sideboard that Michael, the manager, found at a local flea market for only a hundred dollars. Every day, they serve breakfast from it and use it to store extra plates, glasses, and silverware.

BAMBOO REVOLUTION AND COAVA COFFEE ROASTERS

Portland, Oregon
www.bamboorevolution.com
www.coavacoffee.com

Coexisting happily in a 10,000-square-foot warehouse that was once an auto body shop, Bamboo Revolution showroom and Coava Coffee Roasters are showing that through cooperation—sharing costs as well as space—a sense of community can be created. Lately, more and more local businesses are repurposing old warehouses, sharing space, and combining their varied talents to bring in customers. Bamboo Revolution is a bamboo supply company with a design/build division. They renovated their own showroom and created a unique space for the award-winning coffee shop that roasts its own beans onsite.

To fill the large warehouse space and create some industrial-inspired pieces, the designers at Bamboo Revolution brought in functional pieces of large factory equipment and created bamboo tabletops for them—perfect for coffee drinkers to hang out at and mingle around. How fun would it be to have a kitchen island made from an iconic piece of Americana as the base and a gorgeous salvaged top?

▲ The old warehouse had tons of plywood shelving when Bamboo Revolution took it over. Instead of getting rid of it, they used a unique finishing process to create the blackened look of the paneling at the top of the wall. The farmhouse sink in the coffee shop was made by a local company called Eleek, which makes its products from 100% recycled aluminum from sources such as broken window and door screens.

▶ This old drill press, now converted into a table, was found by Keith Shradar, one of the owners of Bamboo Revolution, at a tool-and-equipment supplier. It was from a General Motors building in Michigan and it still works. More and more designers are seeing the unique aesthetic of the industrial style and are using pieces of outdated equipment to make one-of-a-kind dining tables, kitchen islands, nightstands, and more.

▼ Salvaged metal industrial machinery bases and beautiful bamboo tops make for an inspired community table at this coffee shop. The contrasting details are what make these salvaged pieces work so well.

THE STORE

Waitsfield, Vermont

www.vermontstore.com

Waitsfield, Vermont is home to The Store. Built in 1834 as a Methodist meeting house, it was lovingly restored in 1985 by Jackie Rose to house her shop, which had been located on Sugarbush Mountain. With its warm environment, beautifully exposed beams, and wide pine boards covered in antique Oriental rugs, The Store feels more like your grandmother's home than a retail space. It's now run by Jackie's daughter, Kathy, who offers customers coffee or tea upon arrival. The Store sells wonderful gourmet gifts, specialty foods, cookware, and home accessories, and it also has a second floor filled with antiques for sale. Once a children's toy area, the teaching kitchen is a great example of how a working kitchen can include salvaged and vintage pieces. This kind of design works well for any kitchen where the chef rules and guests gather.

▸ To enter the kitchen, you pass through barn-board doors that were made by a local woodworker, Peter Pomerantz. Peter purchased the salvaged boards at Mason Brothers Architectural Salvage. Placed on a new metal slider, they can be opened fully, allowing customers easy access from the store to the kitchen, and closed when a class is in session. The vintage rug at the entrance to the kitchen adds a nice pop of color and texture.

◂◂ An extra-large antique railroad-car luggage rack that Jackie purchased at an auction many years ago was placed over the sink. It not only provides convenient access to the copper pots and pans but also serves as the main decor for the room. Most of the copper pots are vintage, as are the rolling pins. Jackie found the smaller railroad-car luggage racks, which house the cookbooks at the far left in the photo, on eBay. Together, Jackie and her daughter, Kathy, who now runs The Store, created the test kitchen with open shelving and usable copper pots to make the room feel relaxed, spacious, and homey.

The lobby of the Ace Hotel in Portland is simple with bold design features. An exceptionally large coffee table made with recycled tin is surrounded by midcentury office chairs and an oversized L-shaped couch upholstered in fabric made from recycled army ponchos. Vintage letters spelling "hotel" lean against a simple wood wainscoted wall. The plants in the middle of the table create a visual barrier to add a bit of privacy.

◂ Staying in this room feels more like being at a friend's house than in a hotel. Vintage suitcases are used as end tables, old industrial table lamps were turned into wall-mounted sconces, and a vintage leather chair and kilim rug were added to give the room a warm, comfortable feel. The headboard and bed frame are upholstered in the same recycled army-poncho material as the couch in the lobby. The room also incorporates a barn slider with reclaimed wood—except here it covers the window in lieu of a traditional curtain. The painting on the wall is by a local artist.

▾ Each room is laid out differently, but all incorporate salvage material in ingenious ways. This room has a sliding bathroom door, saving space in the room and making an outstanding visual statement. This kind of door is easy to add to any home using reclaimed lumber and a vintage barn slider or even a new one purchased at a feed store. Functional and space-saving, this type of door eliminates the extra space needed for the door to swing open.

THE ACE HOTEL

Portland, Oregon
www.acehotel.com

The Ace Hotel reinvents hospitality. Called "the country's most original new hotel" by the *New York Times*, the Ace appeals to the creative class. Modern bohemian, vintage mod, creative hip—however you describe it, this budget boutique hotel with locations in Seattle, New York City, Portland, Palm Springs, and Los Angeles is leading the way in showing that the hospitality industry can recycle and repurpose materials in exceptional design. Atelier Ace, the award-winning in-house creative team, works with local artisans, architects, and designers in each of their locations. Each property is different, reflecting the area and always putting sustainability at the forefront.

One dramatic statement in each room allows the rest of the room, including the bedding, to be uncomplicated, with clean lines. This vintage movie poster tucked in behind the headboard (again, upholstered with recycled army-poncho material) is all the "wow" this room needs. The blocks of wood that serve as side tables and the reclaimed wood desk in front of the bed add warmth to the room. Movie posters add a vintage mod vibe to any room. Perfect for a bedroom, they could also work well in a midcentury dining room or even an eclectic living room space. I've seen extra-large posters in antique shops, online, and at movie collector booths at fairs.

This room is an excellent example of how salvaged pieces can be reused for different purposes. One metal trunk, low and flat, serves as a coffee table—great for a hotel room, with all the wear and tear. Another functions as a table support, bracing a reclaimed piece of wood. With a vintage turntable and office chair, and state-of-the-art television and phone, the desk is useful for today's traveler, in addition to working as a room divider in place of a wall, which would have made the room feel small and choppy.

Small details count. The headboard and the tissue box are covered in the army-poncho material mentioned earlier. The old desk lamps beside all the beds in the hotel were converted to wall sconces by Rejuvenation, a company that found dozens of these lamps in an old warehouse building. A salvaged block of wood and vintage books serve as end tables. Simple design, recycled material, and use of local craftsman—these are what make the Ace Hotel's creative team stand out as leaders in salvage design.

REJUVENATION

Portland, Oregon
www.rejuvenation.com

Now expanded to locations in Seattle, Los Angeles, and Berkeley, Rejuvenation was founded in Portland in 1977 by Jim Kelly as an architectural salvage shop. It is housed in the historic, 47,000-square-foot Neustadter Building, which for many years served as a wholesale flower mart. Rejuvenation is now part of the Williams-Sonoma family, renowned for its vintage and reproduction period-lighting, it still holds true to its architectural-salvage roots. The stores are filled with displays that include unique salvage pieces, from tables made with industrial pieces to vintage cabinetry and lighting. Their inspiring vignettes prove that castoffs and cool finds can be household treasures.

▲ Vintage deer lawn ornaments, an antique wood table, an industrial metal base turned tree, and a vintage light fixture hanging over the whole ensemble make for a quirky, lively space.

▶ This display uses vintage metal baskets cleverly. These hold rolled up carpets, but you could use them in your own home to hold towels in the bathroom, umbrellas in the entryway, or wood by the fireplace.

◀◀ This vignette at Rejuvenation feels like an elegant dining area with a touch of industrial style. The round table was made from reclaimed wood and an industrial base from an old manufacturing plant. The industrial cabinet in the background would make a great sideboard in a kitchen or entryway. A surveyor's vintage tripod is turned into a one-of-a-kind floor lamp, ideal for an intimate dining setting or living room. Layering vintage rugs is a design idea you can import straight to your own dining room. The numerous period lights hanging above the table are reproductions, but you could easily get this same look with vintage lighting. By displaying their salvaged and new items together in this sort of "vignette" style (rather than in traditional store isles), Rejuvenation offers glimpses of how creative a dining and other rooms can look.

Even from the street you can see the Casa Madrona's extra-large vintage mirror—reflecting the name of the hotel and the trees from outside—and the floor-to-ceiling bookshelves filled with vintage hardcover books. The contemporary fireplace and fabrics give the lobby a feeling of simple elegance with an Old World flavor. The interior designers found the gilded-frame mirror at the Antique & Art Exchange in San Francisco, a very popular antique and collectibles store. A gorgeous statement piece all on its own, it also reflects a significant amount of natural light into the lobby.

◀ Arranged by color, the books are on topics relevant to the area: yachting, the mountains, the redwoods, Sausalito, and more. How did they find all these books? The interior design company used a website called Books by the Foot, which sells used books by the linear foot. They picked out the books by color and topic. Without their jackets, these cloth hardcover books have a more textured, antique look. The other vintage pieces, including the bottle, were found at local antique stores.

▼ Sometimes simpler is better, as this display behind the front desk of the Casa Madrona shows. Lead designer Kim Deetjen found the vintage lifesaving buoy in Charleston, South Carolina, at one of her favorite shops, South of Market. Behind it is a crisp white sail, which makes the vintage piece really stand out. Recycled sails and old lifesaving buoys can be found in a variety of colors and sizes, and they make great wall decorations in any cottage or coastal home.

CASA MADRONA HOTEL & SPA

Sausalito, California
www.casamadrona.com

Casa Madrona is a boutique hotel and spa located in the heart of historic downtown Sausalito, north of San Francisco. Overlooking Richardson Bay, this historic property dates back to 1885, when it was a privately owned mansion. It was converted to a bed and breakfast in 1906 before it became a hotel. In 2010, when MetWest purchased the property and asked Terra Resort Group to manage it, their goal was to restore its status as a world-renowned location, which they did with the help of the team at TruexCullins Architecture and Interior Design. With incredible attention to detail, the stylish interior design includes recycled and salvaged goods, alluding to its heyday of elegant yachting and gracious service.

▲ The Casa Madrona's bathrooms have a clean, nautical look. The green glass shelf that runs above the sink, through the shower glass, and into the shower itself is a GleenGlass product made from 100% recycled post-consumer and postindustrial flat glass. This company's custom made products include no other aggregate or product and are eco-friendly and good for LEED certification.

▶ This close-up shows how their unique, green-hued GleenGlass is manufactured, by joining multiple layers of recycled glass of varying thickness—a process that gives the edge of the shelf a wave-like look. It is used throughout the hotel, including in the spa's steam rooms. GleenGlass is just one type of recycled glass that can be used throughout the bathroom; tiles and other features such as sink counters can be made from a variety of others. Because glass is a nonporous material, it's perfect for bathroom walls and counters. Note also the reusable bottles of shampoo, conditioner, and soap, another trend hotels are turning to.

ABATTOIR

Atlanta, Georgia
www.starprovisions.com

An elegant design with industrial-era edge—that's Abattoir. Owned by chef Anne Quatrano, the restaurant is located in Atlanta's White Provision building, which was built in 1910 as a meat-packing plant in the city's historic district. Today—thanks to the architecture firm Square Feet Studio and interior designer Dominick Coyne—this former slaughterhouse has been transformed into a dining environment unlike any you've ever seen.

With all the big, bold, salvaged finds, including the metal backpacking picking basket, Abattoir's entrance feels well anchored in the large industrial space. The prints on the wall are from an old book, the lamps are vintage posts, and the hostess stand is an old podium. Cleverly put together with warm neutral colors and beautiful fabric curtains, this salvage design makes you feel like you have just arrived at a friend's home.

Design details like those in Abattoir can be transferred to any home. As the wood wall here shows, structural elements can easily play the role of decor as well. The exposed tree rings in the wood itself, the notches in the beams, and the thickness of the wall all contribute to making this structural element a thing of real beauty. The neutral color of the couch and the painted brick allow the wall to visually stand out in the space.

Starting with a whole warehouse of salvaged beams that were over 17 inches square—and, conveniently, a cousin with a wood mill—Anne gathered her team to help her create a restaurant design that recalled the building's past. Five-foot-thick walls were built from 100-year-old heart-pine beams, which were originally from a Goodyear Factory and retained much of their original paint. The design team left the ends of the beams exposed, creating a beautiful patterned texture. The brick walls of the building itself were also left exposed, painted the same color as the old country-store counter that now serves as the hostess desk.

By cleverly arranging separate dining areas, the designers managed to make the very large space feel quaint and intimate. This section of the restaurant, with a long vintage table and modern leather bench, is for a large group. Along with a wall of vintage ladles, an extra-large vintage bowl serves as the decor. At the end of the table another vintage beam wall both separates the dining areas and gives the table a stunning backdrop. This setting could be easily transferred to a home with a long, narrow dining area.

Oversized vintage mirrors line the brick wall, reflecting light from the rest of the space as well as giving each customer a view of the vintage light fixtures and center-room decor. In keeping with the rest of the space, another solid 5-foot wall of reclaimed heart pine (which is on the floors as well) separates the dining areas from the bathroom. On the wall to the right you can see the same beams, this time in a vertical wainscoting position. Same material in three locations—floor, wall, beams—three totally different looks.

▲ Simple, simple, simple—yet as stunning as it gets! This vintage three-faucet enameled cast-iron sink makes a real statement. The simplicity of the rest of the design allows the sink to be the focal point. When designing with salvage, it's important not to have a bunch of strong elements fighting for attention. This bathroom shows you how it's done right.

▶ Even small details can add a huge amount of character to a room. Here, vintage industrial mechanical lamps were turned into bar pendants, and an extra-large basket is used for the center light.

◀◀ Takingcenter stage in the restaurant is an old metal machinist's table. Aesthetically attractive and functionally useful, it serves as the wait station, holding plates, water, napkins, and other table needs in beautiful vintage buckets, baskets, and a large wooden trough. It also serves as a room divider, again eliminating the need for walls. Many homeowners choose to design their homes similarly. This table could easily serve as a kitchen island with overhead pendants, separating the kitchen from the dining and living areas. Hanging above the table are two vintage metal "dipping baskets" once used for refinishing silver. Designer Dominick Coyne had them turned into light fixtures.

This building is just one of the many structures on the property that are geared toward entertaining. Made with salvaged wood from a neighbor's barn, including the barn doors and windows, it is romantic in an understated way.

MT. HOOD BED AND BREAKFAST

Parkdale, Oregon
www.mthoodbnb.com

Tucked away in a small Oregon town on the edge of Mt. Hood is a delightful bed and breakfast that hosts many weddings. Owners Mike and Jackie Rice take a very hands-on approach to running the place, including making many of the buildings and outbuildings themselves. The Rices also focus on using reclaimed and salvage material to build and decorate their structures. In fact, when an old barn on an adjacent property was going to be burned down by the local fire department as a training session, Mike and Jackie asked the property owners

Sometimes a fresh coat of paint is called for—and sometimes it's not. Along with the old, peeling paint on these recycled single-pane windows, the unique character of the different salvaged boards that serve as the counter gives this building a romantic, Old World feeling.

The remodeled rooms in the inn have vintage furniture that has been reupholstered. In addition, this room includes a sliding barn board door made from salvaged wood for the bathroom, and a clever clothes rack on the wall made from an old piece of wood and vintage doorknobs. This classic, clean aesthetic shows that an inn doesn't have to look outdated when it incorporates salvaged and vintage products.

if they could take the barn boards before the rest of the structure was burned. Forever grateful to their neighbors for saying yes, the Rices have been using the salvaged old-growth wood for a variety of projects ever since. Filled with personality, this inn, with exceptional views of Mt. Hood, gardens, orchards, and fields of swaying grass, is an excellent example of how simple it is to add character with salvage in your home or in backyard structures.

◂ This do-it-yourself family wanted a fun bar area for their guests. Using more of the salvaged barn wood, they put together an inviting outdoor cocktail area. The wood was left in its natural state and the vintage wine barrels make excellent tables.

▾ A beautifully displayed collection of vintage bottles and silver trays sits on top of the antique armoire in the dining room. To add soft lighting to the room, Jackie tucked in some small white holiday lights behind the bottles. They not only provide a softer ambience for dinner or breakfast but also enhance the beauty of the vintage glass. This type of display would look great in a bedroom or on a mantel or sideboard in a dining room.

▸▸ This lighting display takes up most of the ceiling in the barn. Hung from a vintage wagon wheel, the romantic paper-ball lighting and swag fabric are stunning. It's an idea that could easily be adapted to other styles, too—you could hang industrial lamps, Edison bulbs on cloth wire, or numerous recycled chandeliers all painted the same color from an old wagon wheel.

SELECT DESIGN

Burlington, Vermont
www.selectdesign.com

Select Design, located in an old industrial building in Burlington, Vermont, is a business that specializes in brand development for teams, companies, and events across the globe. When they designed their office space, they decided to enhance the building's industrial past rather than hide it. In 1921 the building was home to the Vermont Milk Chocolate Company. After many other businesses came and went, Select Design moved in, designing the space to incorporate salvaged parts and pieces from the original building and the variety of business that it has housed.

DESIGN TIP

Finding a local fabricator who works with recycled metals is a great place to start when looking for unusual shapes of salvaged metal. Whether it is for a wall hanging, a table base, or a unique door handle, scrap metal pieces are an easy addition to your salvage repertoire.

A piece of a 1956 Buick hangs from chains on the wall in the first-floor conference room. This is just one of the many salvaged features that this forward-thinking company's owners, Kevin and Jeff, used to make their space a fun, creative place for employees to work in and customers to visit.

◂◂ When you walk into the building and are greeted at the reception desk, you can't help but smile, especially with the oversized scrap metal art hanging on the brick wall, smiling back. The metal pieces were picked up at Queen City Steel, a local metal company and fabricator who also recycles scrap metal.

The industrial sliding doors that flank the entryway to the third-floor conference room were found in the basement of the building. Used as fire doors by a past company, they are made from three layers of oak, cross-laminated and clad with leaded sheet metal, and were brought back to life as a key design feature in Select Design's space.

Repurposed into a workstation for the design crew, this old metal door once served as a hatch on a roof.

▸▸ The tabletop here was once a door of a popular Burlington bar called Nectar's. The table legs were constructed in the same way as the vintage sliding fire doors. Select Design's owners, Kevin and Jeff, love the stories behind the materials and the imaginative ways they are now used in their offices, helping to keep everyone happy and creative.

Tracee is grabbing a glass behind her bar, which is made from wood from an old barn in Oregon. The top of the bar was planed and given a glossy finish, the sides were left rough-cut and oiled, and the shelves were left in their natural, weathered, rough-cut state—one salvaged barn, three different looks. Even the salvaged beam in the middle was left in its natural state, showing off the broken edge. The vintage beer tap she found from a friend.

CORKSCREW WINE BAR

Portland, Oregon
www.corkscrewpdx.com

Tracee Danyluk, owner of the Corkscrew Wine Bar, loves all things salvage. Her husband founded Portland's largest rebuild center, so when it came time to design her wine bar, it was no surprise that unique salvaged material played a key role. With the help of local builders, artisans, and friends, Tracee created a wine bar that is not only inviting but very unique. For the Corkscrew, Tracee wanted the space to feel like the inside of a wine barrel with warm woods. Goal accomplished!

▸ All the table bases in the bar are made from old sewing machines (she only used ones that were no longer working). The tops of the sewing machines were salvaged and given to a friend who uses them for styling props. The vintage wood on the tables and walls came from the barn the bar was made from. The tables were planed and given a glossy varnish and the walls were oiled and left in a natural rough cut. The window is made from leftover pulley wheels from the sewing machines.

▾ Tracee created shelving by the front door to display some of her wine. These salvaged boards, from the same barn, were left in their natural rough-cut state with no finish, which is why they have a gray, weathered look.

DESIGN TIP

The look of this wine bar is just one example of how many different ways there are to finish salvaged wood. You can plane it, leave it rough-cut, or lightly sand it. Finishing options are equally varied—waxed, natural, painted, whitewashed, stained, or even decoupaged! Wood is one of the most versatile kinds of salvaged material available. Many of the older barns that are falling down are made from old-growth timber, a better quality and stronger wood than most virgin wood today. Harvesting old barn wood or any other type of salvaged wood takes some knowledge and experience. Many experts in the reclaimed-wood field can help you find the right type for your project.

This vignette is just one of dozens set up for Sweet Salvage's monthly four-day event. The designers of each vignette are on hand to answer questions about the salvage material, how they displayed it, as well as the stories behind the goods. Chock full of fantastic finds, the vignettes are a feast for the eyes.

SWEET SALVAGE

Phoenix, Arizona
www.sweetsalvage.net

Sweet Salvage, in Phoenix, Arizona, is open only four days a month, and when the doors are unlocked on that first day, long lines of designers and creative homeowners snake all the way down the street. Inside, dealers and designers sell vintage and antique goods in beautifully styled displays. Each vignette is created in a way that makes it easy for designers and homeowners to replicate that exact look in their own home or project. Plus, each month the store has a theme—French country, holiday, secret garden, farmhouse, Park Avenue, and so on. Many attendees go not only for the salvage and antique products but also for the inspiring display ideas.

▲ Kim Rawlins and Katie Hibbs, owners of Sweet Salvage, are preparing the store for another event. Although the store is only open a few days a month, it takes them (and other designers) weeks to get the displays ready for the public. The materials are cleaned, painted, repaired, and then beautifully displayed. Kim and Katie encourage homeowners to take pictures, copy the display ideas, and get creative themselves with salvaged goods.

▸ This holiday-themed vignette is geared toward natural and cream colors, greenery, and organic-looking textiles. The vintage iron gate hanging from the ceiling and holding an old bucket is just one of hundreds of items that inspire design and decorating ideas.

With only 800 square feet for a staff of six in the entire office, the room that Jessica and another designer work in also serves as the reception area. Jessica's desk, made from a cut of locally felled myrtle wood, is a stunning design piece. The living edge, splits, and shape reveal the character of the original tree. The basket under the desk, which serves as a wastebasket, is an Asian antique. The old French wine basket and bottle in the corner hint to Jessica's European roots. The wall decor is simply made with old printer blocks, arranged in a pattern that makes for a striking art piece.

◂◂ Bathed in natural light streaming in from extra-large windows, the vintage drafting table serves as a conference table for Jessica, her team, and their clients. It's also a great place to lay out blueprints and drawings while designs are being planned. The retro-style red chairs, from the 1980s, are not only functional but also play a key role in the aesthetic of the room, allowing the rest of the space to be kept simple and white.

◂ Jessica and her husband, Yianni Doulis, an architect, assembled this mirror display using salvage mirrors cut to form a mosaic pattern. The jigsaw-like display makes the bathroom sparkle and feel bigger than it really is.

JESSICA HELGERSON INTERIOR DESIGN

Portland, Oregon
www.jhinteriordesign.com

Don't let the small size of Jessica Helgerson's interior design office in Portland, Oregon, fool you. Her team of talented designers has some of the biggest and freshest ideas in the industry today, and much of it includes sustainable and salvaged materials. Recycled wood, retro furnishing, and vintage finds are just a few of the salvaged items that Jessica's team incorporates into the designs. Whether she's remodeling a 1920s Mediterranean-style home with retro furnishing reupholstered in bright oranges or a historic Gothic Revival with glass and black furnishings, Jessica has an eye for her clients' needs while holding fast to her commitment to green building and sustainability. This commitment is reflected in her own office space, which is simple, efficient, and filled with salvage finds.

DESIGN TIP

Use of "felled" wood is a new and growing trend. As salvaged wood has grown in popularity, more and more city officials are making sure that trees that fall on public and private properties (such as into streets and such) are not sent directly to the wood chipper anymore. Many of these trees, which often fall due to storms, are gorgeous, durable, sought-after species that you don't see on the market today. Black acacia, myrtle, walnut—these are just a few of the types that are recovered. Furniture makers, artisans, and building companies are buying these felled trees from the city. This not only creates jobs in the area but also helps the city reduce its disposal costs—not to mention giving the once-majestic trees a new life as one-of-a-kind pieces of furniture.

The Hourglass Bar is a great place to relax after a long day on the slopes. With its mixture of contemporary design and rustic elegance, including the stump tables created by local woodworker Parker Nichols and his team at Vermont Wildwoods, the space feels warm and welcoming. Although the stump table looks like a simple project, months of preparation went into its manufacture. On a drive one day Parker spotted an ash tree that had been struck by lightning and fallen. He asked the owner of the property if he could buy the fallen tree and then he cut it up and let it dry outside for 2 months. After it was sent to a kiln for 3 weeks, the top was ground flat, the bark was removed, and the entire piece was sanded. Finally, a two-part epoxy was applied to the top, and one layer was brushed down the sides. Other wood stumps are scattered throughout the bar, including one extra-large maple—almost 5 feet high and about 14 feet wide—that serves as the hostess stand.

STOWE MOUNTAIN LODGE

Stowe, Vermont
www.stowemountainlodge.com

At the Stowe Mountain Lodge—a world-class resort at the edge of Mount Mansfield in Vermont—the staff and lodge owners are committed to the longstanding New England tradition of combining a welcoming graciousness with a respect for environment. The luxury lodge proves that you can incorporate local artisan traditions with salvaged materials and embrace contemporary design all at the same time.

▲ Solstice, the lodge's signature restaurant with panoramic views of the mountainside, has oversized columns along the edge of the buffet stand. The columns are covered in recycled glass tile made from wine bottles. The tile in front of the open kitchen (to the right) is also made from recycled glass. Butcher-block tables are all custom made from wood that was salvaged from the property itself. With its mix of rustic and contemporary features, this fine-dining restaurant shows that using salvaged material doesn't mean sacrificing elegance.

▶ When nature gives you details as spectacular as those here, there's no need for much else. To highlight the natural beauty of this table's wood, the artisan cut it into pieces of various sizes, glued the pieces together, then cut the whole thing to get a round shape, and finally sealed it with a high-gloss finish. The arresting pattern of tree rings makes this table a piece of art. Using local artisans to create the pieces not only perpetuates traditions but also helps the local economy.

▲ The recycled glass tile used in the columns in the restaurant was used throughout the spa area as well. The art on the wall, whose design recalls the tree rings of the stump tables and dining tables, is made of metal. A highly recycled product, metal is an interesting element to add because it is unexpected. As I showed earlier, salvaged metal, especially in old industrial forms, is being used more frequently, but the approach taken here—a flat sheet with a sand-blasted effect—is also inventive.

◂◂ A vintage sink, shelving made from salvaged pallets, rolling islands made of salvaged material, and a vintage sign picked up in Alaska where the homeowner's children were born, are a few of the finds in this home's creative remodel. Kerri Hoyt-Pack's story is just one of many in this chapter on how individuals have styled and designed with salvage.

Salvage Success Stories

While gathering information across the country for my books, I discovered hundreds of exceptional salvage design stories: a tiny old garage transformed into a beautiful home; a glamorous all-white New York City apartment; a colorful Bohemian-style house on the beaches of Georgia; and a Phoenix ranch house given an eclectic Western style, to name a few. These salvage success stories—and many more—are featured in this chapter.

During the course of my travels and book research, I learned a few important things. First, the story behind the salvage material or piece is very important to the homeowners. They enjoy the history of the salvage as much as they enjoy the look itself.

Shannon Quimby is all about fun—in her home, design, and life. She and her family enjoy a home filled with salvaged material that's used both structurally and as decor (see p. 185). Here, Shannon and I relax after a long photo shoot, enjoying a fire in the salvaged brick fireplace that backs up to the one inside the house. You'll see more pictures of this elegant home later in the chapter.

Second, they embrace *wabi sabi*—the Japanese worldview that focuses on the acceptance of transience and imperfection. For these homeowners and their spaces, nothing is perfect, which makes it . . . well, *perfect*. It's a comfortable and accepting way to live.

Third, these folks love like-minded salvage gurus. They talk passionately about flea market finds and other exciting salvage scores. Together they form a community all their own, always welcoming newcomers with open arms.

Fourth, the number of different ways that homeowners experiment and use materials is mind-boggling. Neckties are turned into flags, driftwood into headboards, maps into cabinet fronts, industrial machinery parts into kitchen shelving, scuba tanks into lights—the list goes on and on.

And last but not least, putting it all together is the fun part. The goal, of course, is always to create a great space, but for these homeowners, it's the hunt for the materials, the search for the deal, the discovery of that perfect vintage light fixture or the history behind the table that all come together to tell a story. Their love of the process was evident, coming through clearly in designs that are inviting, varied, and charming.

Hearing homeowners (and designers) passionately describe how they came across a particular salvaged piece is one of the most inspiring aspects of working in this business. Whether the piece was found in a thrift shop, custom made from repurposed material, plucked from the side of the road, or once resided in a historic hotel, the stories are endlessly diverse.

For many of these people, using reclaimed material in their decor as well as their architectural design is a no-brainer. Some just added a few salvaged details to their homes, such as recycled glass turned into pendants over a kitchen island, whereas others planned their entire home or renovation around the salvage "look." Regardless of the extent to which salvaged materials were used, however, these homeowners were inspired by the history of the reclaimed materials they found, sometimes by their own travels, and by making environmentally conscious choices for their family and home.

This chapter takes a closer peek at some of these stories, revealing the sheer variety of styles that salvage design can offer and, hopefully, providing a useful portfolio of design ideas for *your* own home.

HUNTING AND GATHERING

San Rafael, California

Tricia Rose and her husband, Stefan Sargent, take the concept of "cottage industry" to a whole new level. They live and work (Tricia owns a natural bedding and flax linen company called Rough Linen, and Stefan makes corporate videos and documentaries) in a 1930s duck hunting cabin perched on piers over the water in San Rafael, California. The small cottage is part of an eclectic bohemian neighborhood near San Francisco. Tricia and Stefan have slowly updated the space with a thoughtful combination of found, made, and vintage objects. With views of the Marin Islands and Richmond–San Raphael Bridge, and a deck overlooking the water, it's a perfect place to work and play.

◂◂ Tricia Rose picks up neglected furniture with good bones and even wades out from the breakwater to collect wood drifting in the waves. Whether it comes from nature or is an heirloom piece, she knows just how to fix it or display it in her home. The dining room walls are planked with reclaimed wood scrubbed with a solution of ferrous sulfate made from white vinegar and steel wool (when combined, the vinegar and steel wool create a chemical reaction that darkens wood). Tricia framed an extra large mirror with a beam she found on the beach. The beam was originally 6 inches deep; with the help of her sons, she took it to a local mill, where it was sliced and rebated to fit around the mirror. The lights above the salvaged dining table and chairs are old crab traps that were left on the property when they bought it. The lifesaver, metal basket, and ship's copper ventilators used as wall sconces were gathered from different sources, including the side of the freeway. Sunshine from skylights and windows on two sides reflects in the mirror, helping keep this room light and airy as well as adding even more depth to the rough-textured walls.

◂ Most of the cabinetry in the kitchen is original but updated with vintage maps on the doors. Each map has a personal connection to Tricia's family history. Ever resourceful, Tricia made the counter's backsplash from the packing crate that the counter arrived in. With a coat of paint, it adds another textural element to the kitchen. Even the refrigerator is paneled with rough planking and lined with a salvaged piece of lattice. The china tea set is a family heirloom from Scotland.

▲ Nearby beaches, the marina, and a long breakwater provide abundant salvaged wood for furniture and crafts, all of it worn and weathered by sea, salt, and marine creatures. Tricia likes simple design best and this guest bedroom shows it. The headboard consists of planks that Tricia painted and attached to the wall. Paired with bedding from her own line, the soothing colors make for a peaceful sleeping experience.

◀ On the old covered porch, Tricia painted the tile floors in large diagonal checks of cream and gray, and she slipcovered twin sofas in her company's rough linen. Vintage laundry baskets serve as side tables—she spotted them at the Waterloo Station in England and the station manager put her in touch with the basketmaker, who still makes them. Behind the couch is an extra-large mirror framed in driftwood that reflects the sky and the water into the space, making it feel larger than it is. The horizontal wainscoting was original to the cottage, which once was covered in layers of pressed board and drywall.

▶▶ The master bedroom headboard is a tour de force of salvaged driftwood. Tricia likes the fact that the old wood has been floating in salt water, which gets rid of any bugs, leaving it thoroughly clean and smooth. The simple, wall-mounted lamps have been giving a little extra style with old fishing nets over the shades. Vintage maps, salvaged side tables, and, of course, her own natural flax rough-linen bedding finish off the space.

Tricia repurposed walnut Ikea benches into cabinet doors. White walls, noble woods (walnut, teak, mahogany, and oak), baskets, and fishing netting over the window give the room a boat-like feel. Tricia loves her workshop of power tools, calling them "a girl's best friend." Her expertise in using them allows her to be creative with salvaged material and repurposed furniture.

Following the scrap-paneling scheme in the living room, painted and unpainted planking was used to line the walls and ceiling in the master bedroom. Tricia had initially intended to paint all of the planking, but the varied look of the scrap wood she found goes so well with the striped linen curtains that she's contemplating keeping it piebald, at least for now. She sanded down the old dresser and added rope for handles. The vintage pulleys and stanchions on the dresser are from a sailing neighbor. An old teak deck chair covered by a Gotland fleece sits in the corner. The industrial light hanging from the wall, hooked on an old railroad tie, bounces light off the wood beautifully.

When the San Francisco nights get chilly, the woodstove makes for a comfortable sitting area. (And there's always plenty of scrap wood!) Tricia reupholstered the old armchair in gray flannel. The narrow walls on either side of the woodstove are also paneled, and the long, narrow paintings (one hangs sideways) balance the space. The vintage metal trunk is just one of many Tricia has collected over the years, as there's little storage space in the cabin.

◂ Digging through hundreds of old desks and shelves at a used-office-supply warehouse, Rosanne found a credenza that fit perfectly under her window for use as a mini-bar. I showed up for a visit and, spotting a potential DIY project, I promptly sanded down and refinished the wood top and gave the dull, office-gray hardware a quick fix with some metal spray paint. By removing a few drawers, I created an open space to display their vintage soda bottles and cocktail mixes. The drawers are perfect for coasters, wine books, glasses, and cocktail napkins. An old wooden frame picked up from a local secondhand shop was a perfect fit for the metal letters a friend had given her.

▾ For the wall behind the tub, Rosanne used marble tile pieces left over from another project, cutting them in half and installing them vertically. This clever idea is a good reminder that salvaged tile can be cut in many shapes and patterns. She picked up the vintage silk window curtain at a reuse store and repurposed it as a shower curtain. The wooden rack that holds the extra toilet paper was once part of an old sewing machine drawer, and the rod it hangs on was an extra curtain rod she had in the house. The vintage gnome pulls it all together.

TWIN PASSIONS

Portland, Oregon

The passion for salvage often runs in the family, and that holds true for me, too. My twin sister, Rosanne, and her husband, Sean, have great style—modern and hip. When they first moved into their 1926 Georgian brick home in northeast Portland, the kitchen, bathrooms, and dining area hadn't been updated since the 1950s. Using lots of unique salvage touches and a nod to the era of the house, they remodeled it while bringing in modern comfort.

The light fixtures above the island in this remodeled kitchen were made from glass pieces found at the non-profit ReBuilding Center in Portland, Oregon. With electrical components added by a lighting expert, they make stunning pendants. The vintage Bertoia bar stools were found on eBay. Pulling the look together are the small details of vintage vases, cutting boards, an old milk carrier, and bar glasses.

This dining room design proves that you have to look in more than one place to create a space. The chandelier is a family heirloom from Rosanne's husband. Beneath it is a farmhouse table that Rosanne spotted at a second-hand shop whose proceeds go toward helping homeless families find housing. Of course, looking for the perfect piece can take time, but it's worth the wait. Until she comes across the perfect dining room chairs, these metal folding ones bought at a garage sale will work fine. The wall sconces, found at the ReBuilding Center, are a great reminder that salvaged pieces aren't always old—these were new, lying in a pile at the rebuild center. Rosanne drilled a hole in the back to create a sconce, removed the lamp canopy, and gave it a modern look with an exposed Edison-style bulb. The fantastic orange metal pieces at the end of the room were once used in a car-mechanic shop. Rosanne found them at Seek the Unique, another of her favorite shops in Portland. Above the orange cabinets are some fun chalkboard frames that I created from Goodwill finds during one of my visits (step-by-step instructions for the project can be found under "chalk picture frame" on the DIY NETWORK online).

▲ This cozy kitchen nook has some interesting salvaged pieces. For the tabletop, Rosanne had leftover marble from their countertops cut into a bistro-table-sized circle. Foam camping cushions covered with an old fleece blanket were used for the bench. The leftover pieces of the blanket became bows around a few of the pillows.

▲ During one of my visits, Rosanne and I found an old dresser (left photo) to convert into a bathroom vanity. We sanded the cabinet completely and then cut holes in the top for the new sinks and faucets. The dresser handles were sprayed silver with a metal paint to match the fixtures. We painted the whole thing with a high-gloss paint to make it water-resistant. Along with the floor tiles from the 1920s and the mod oval mirror, this dresser gives the bathroom a funky old-school look. Complementing the dresser-turned-vanity is a small antique white table (right photo) and a vintage vase and bowl. Simple and elegant, this design lets the history of the bathroom speak for itself.

▲▲ Old industrial letters picked up at Rejuvenation add a little charm and humor to the guest powder room.

▲ The goods in the pantry can be seen through the salvaged French doors that Rosanne picked up at the ReBuilding Center. She painted them, put on some hinges, and added magnets to keep the doors from swinging open. The old oil painting of flowers, in the foreground, was found at Goodwill.

▲▲ Most people can't wait to get rid of their 1970s light fixtures, but with a little creativity, you can bring them back to life. That's just what Rosanne did with this old bathroom light fixture when she flipped it sideways, painted the base black, and added a pull switch. Hung in the stairwell, it's a perfect fit for the narrow space between the windows.

◀ In the entryway, Rosanne placed a vintage cabinet she picked up at antique flea market. She painted it a high-gloss black and lined the inside with vintage-looking velvet fabric. Displayed inside are some of their favorite hats—creating a functional as well as aesthetic piece. On top of the cabinet are some more modern salvage finds from local flea markets.

▸ This wine cellar was decorated with lots of salvaged finds, including the tabletop itself, which used to be a beam in the basement. Cut and planed, the beam is now a functional wine bar.

▾ The basement family room shows off great decorating detail. The television can be instantly hidden with a beautiful piece of salvaged wood on a barn slider. The old wood has exceptional detail itself (worm holes, notches, coloring, and more) and doesn't need anything else to create a style.

The master bedroom is a quiet space with whites, metallic silver, and crystal. Kelly found the vintage chair on eBay and had it reupholstered in silver faux leather. The midcentury lacquered side table is one of a pair she spotted at a local antique shop. For the bedroom closet, Kelly painted a couple of salvaged doors white and covered the glass panes with mirrors to hide the contents of the closet and draw more light into the room. The chandelier above the bed is made from a variety of salvaged crystal parts that she picked out and had assembled into a fixture.

GLAMOUR IN THE BIG APPLE

New York, New York

Although Kelly Giesen had spent years antiquing with her mother, it wasn't until she lived on her own in a Baltimore townhouse that she thought about buying architectural antiques or salvage material. The townhouse "had good bones but was a bit boring, as all the original details were gone," Kelly explained. "So I started to add the character back in by renovating with old architectural materials. I was absolutely hooked after that." Now an interior designer living in New York City, Kelly has turned her passion for salvage into a full-time occupation.

Kelly's one-bedroom on the Upper West Side shows us just how to do salvage-glam. She bought the 9x3-foot wreath doors flanking the fireplace from

Elegant and refined, this New York City apartment is a testament to the fact that salvage doesn't have to look old, rustic, or even country. Homeowner and interior designer Kelly Giesen is in love with salvage, and before she designs a space or even takes down a wall, she stockpiles salvage materials—old doors, chandeliers, fireplaces, and even furniture found at antique stores and on eBay. Kelly's living room chairs and couch are all salvaged pieces she had reupholstered in elegant blues and creams as well as in fun fabrics like faux silver leather. She loves the curves and sizes of the older pieces, especially the kidney-bean-shaped couch and the barrel-back chairs she found for $68 at an upstate New York antique shop. The dealer had the price marked "firm"—and that was okay by Kelly!

The wreath door that leads into the bathroom is the same as those in the living room, but here Kelly added beveled mirrors on both sides, giving the bathroom the privacy it needs. She left the top wreath window alone and through it you can see the midcentury chandelier in the bathroom. The three vintage doors can all be seen in the same open space, with the bathroom door reflecting the living space and the natural light. The insides of the kitchen cabinets are also mirrored in the back and reflect the vintage glassware inside them. The pantry doors on the right are salvaged wardrobe doors. Kelly gives her salvage materials a refined look with a coat of white paint. She believes it not only gives them a clean look but it pulls all the pieces together, no matter how different they may be.

Kelly picked up seven vintage wardrobe doors at Demolition Depot, using two of them as bathroom linen-closet doors, one as the tub surround (it was cut to fit), two as the pantry doors in the kitchen, and two for a coat closet. Already an elegant addition to the bathroom, they became even more glamorous with Kelly's addition of circular mirrors and chunky mid-century Lucite knobs. The sink vanity base is a repurposed metal hall console, and the Sputnik light fixture is one of many midcentury lights that enhance the apartment's traditional bones. Kelly found the large Venetian-style mirror in an antique store and spent months deliberating about whether to purchase it, despite knowing it might not be there the next time she stopped in. Fortunately it hadn't been sold by the time she made her decision—it gracefully accentuates the height of the ceiling and opens up the space of the room.

With only word of mouth of her work, Kelly is now is a full-time interior designer. Some of her favorite spots to scavenge for salvage are Olde Good Things, Demolition Depot, and eBay and other online shops—plus, of course, local antique shops. On weekends she peruses flea markets in the city, including one at 77th and Columbus Avenue and another at 25th Street and 6th Avenue.

Demolition Depot before she'd even moved into her current apartment, thinking she could lean them against her living room wall as decor. But they wouldn't fit into the elevator of that apartment building, and they were too heavy to take up 10 flights of stairs. They sat in storage until she found her current apartment, where they fortunately fit beautifully. Kelly added a new door opening on the right side of the fireplace and increased the height of the opening on the left to add the doors. Now the apartment feels much larger and more open, and lots of light streams into the bedroom from the large living room window.

The century-old marble fireplace and metal surround was once in the Plaza Hotel—Kelly got her hands on it when a part of the hotel was being converted into condominiums. She built out the wall a bit to accommodate the recessed television and create the illusion of a real fireplace. Although the fireplace does not actually function, it centers the space visually.

The hanging light fixture was a truly spectacular find. While shopping at the Antique Showplace, Kelly saw a box in a corner with some crystals and metal arms sticking out of a bag. She knew at once it was a vintage Metropolitan Opera fixture because of its unique shape, and she bought it on the spot without even checking to see if all the pieces were there. It took her a day to reassemble it—time she realized was well spent when the fixture came together in its entirety.

Tying all the rooms together is the kitchen/dining space. In the middle of the space is a table with a salvaged-wood top made by Olde Good Things, which not only sells salvage goods but also makes tables and tabletops to size. Kelly placed the salvaged-wood top on a repurposed metal console base she had, and because it was a little low she added a piece of Lucite to raise it up a bit. The chair at the end is a second-hand midcentury swivel chair; Kelly pulled the fabric off the back and reupholstered the seat. The light fixtures are also midcentury pieces and the pantry and closet doors are part of the seven wardrobe doors mentioned earlier. All the glassware and canisters are vintage pieces that she has collected over the years.

Influenced by Donald Judd's furniture in Marfa, Texas (where she once owned an adobe home), Jennifer made this bookshelf herself, using planks of wood discarded by the owners of the Brewery Art Lofts, a Los Angeles live-work community that she once resided in. Leftover construction materials were often stockpiled near her loft and she would make use of what she considered salvageable. These solid pieces of redwood were cut with a jigsaw, and the notches to hold the shelves were chiseled by hand. Jennifer acquired the midcentury couch, chairs, side tables, and lamps by bartering with a furniture-dealer friend and scouring various antique shops. The painting is by Justin Beal, a Los Angeles–based artist.

NOT YOUR AVERAGE ADDITION

Venice, California

Designer Jennifer Siegal, Founder and Principal of Office of Mobile Design, is known for utilizing portable and prefabricated architecture to create ecologically sound, dynamic structures. When she added a 200-square-foot addition to her 800-square-foot 1920s stucco-box-style home in Venice, California, it didn't surprise any-

An antique rug bought in Morocco and some midcentury vintage finds, including chairs and a coffee table, make this moving-truck trailer a comfortable guestroom and place to relax. The addition also added a bit of storage space.

This salvaged moving-truck trailer was repurposed as an addition to designer Jennifer Siegal's California home. The trailer was craned over the house, set on railroad ties, and positioned to look out on the garden and provide easy access to Jennifer's old-Hollywood-style spa area. The original metal loading doors were replaced with large steel-framed glass doors (the original hinges and hardware were reused). The vintage metal chair and table are a great place to read the paper as the sun comes up in the morning.

one that the addition was a recycled drop-frame moving-truck trailer. Only $1500 and already outfitted with mahogany wood floors, the salvaged trailer added a lovely guest bedroom and yoga space in Jennifer's home. Thinking outside the box—or, in this case, *inside* it—Jennifer shows that creative salvaging doesn't have to end at smaller items like doors, beams, and windows.

▲ An original Wedgewood stove (which are very popular now and can be found online or at salvage centers), in the house when Jennifer purchased it in 2002, is a centerpiece of the kitchen. She traded the 1930s Sunbeam model T-9 toaster for a design consultation. On the walls is artwork by her father, Sydney Siegal, along with original prayer paintings from Baja, Mexico, where she and her friends own a trailer at Angel's Camp, which looks out over the ocean. Coffee pots from Italy, spoons from Africa and South America—Jennifer's kitchen is visual record of her world travels.

▶ Following her mantra of keeping things simple, Jennifer used white powder-coated steel for the bathroom counter and window frame, as well as for the structural plate that masks the sink plumbing. Metal is a great, affordable recycled product, and depending on how it's finished, it doesn't have to make a space feel cold. The ceramic sink is from Ikea and the faucet is a high-end Grohe (similar salvaged sinks and faucets can be found at a rebuild center or online). With calming cream-colored tile on the floors, walls, and open shower area, and a large window looking out onto the backyard and vegetable garden, the bathroom feels like an outdoor shower.

◀ The bed frame is made of salvaged steel pieces that Jennifer put together herself after learning how to weld. Its clean lines go nicely with the midcentury black lacquer dresser by Paul McCobb Planner Group—a hand-me-down from Jennifer's parents.

▲ The back wall of the dining area is made from Kirei Board (meaning "pretty flower" in Japanese)—an environmentally friendly substitute for wood, manufactured from reclaimed sorghum straw. The dual swinging glass doors leading out into the garden were originally the entrance to an East L.A. grocery store.

▶ In the main house, the custom-made door is framed with salvaged steel, and the laminated, translucent glass allows a great deal of sun into the space, as well as creating its own design in shadows. The artwork hung throughout the house is by artist Sydney Siegal, Jennifer's father.

Shannon Quimby's kitchen is filled with material salvaged from the bungalow that once stood on the very same spot. The knobs on the upper cabinets are old porcelain electrical insulators. The countertop is concrete with recycled glass, and the wainscoting on the island is from the old bungalow's baseboard interior trim. The wood on the mini-refrigerator door is the old tongue-and-groove Douglas fir flooring—with the original paint (they just scrubbed off the dirt and sealed it). The blue canning jars, bowling pins, cutting board, glasses, bowls, and signs are all vintage or antique. The light fixture over the sink is missing its shade, but Shannon loved the structure of the frame. The enamelware scale, cleverly used as a fruit bowl, was found at an estate sale—buried in a back workshop and with an inch of sawdust on it. (Fortunately, nothing escapes Shannon's keen eye.)

The island top is a combination of the 88-year-old framing from the original home and the leftover new dimensional lumber used in the framing of the new house—another great example of how easy it is to combine old and new. The floors are reclaimed California chestnut, left over from other building jobs and picked up at Green Depot. Board widths ranging from 2 to 5 inches—and lengths from 1 to 5 feet—add a lively character.

NO DUMPSTER NEEDED

Portland, Oregon

Shannon Quimby is a renaissance woman. A do-it-yourself expert, a columnist and photo stylist for national publications, an interior designer for homes and restaurants, a blogger, an HGTV alumnus of two shows, and the author of *Color, Create, Decorate*—she knows her salvage. So when she and her husband, Glenn, bought a corner lot in their neighborhood with a neglected 1920s bungalow that was beyond repair, they didn't think twice about tearing it down and building their dream home—without the use of a single dumpster!

The two gates above the master bed have a story all their own. In 1962, Portland suffered one of its most severe storms, and one of many things that were blown down was an old fence. A resourceful horseman salvaged the boards and made a jumping fence from them. Years later they ended up in a restaurant with a Western decor. After the restaurant closed, the pieces were in storage for 10 years, until one day when a chef who saw them asked if he could have them for his driveway gates. When Shannon and Glenn bought the beat-up bungalow, the gates were still guarding the driveway.

The rest of the room has lots of salvaged features, including reclaimed chestnut flooring, a vintage chair re-covered in coffee-bean sacks, vintage bamboo shelves, an old window with original painting, and 1970s decorative metal pieces from old awnings.

▲ Following the "reuse everything" rule was particularly difficult when it came to finding places for the large amount of interior window, door, and baseboard trim from the original house—all of which was in various widths and colors. But Shannon isn't one to shy from a challenge. In this guest powder room, she used the trim to create a distinct ceiling, reflected in the mirror. The former back door became the vanity, and an old window was turned into the bathroom mirror. An old Danish wooden shoe sits on the concrete-and-recycled-glass countertop; the rest of Shannon's collection of wooden shoes is on display on the back wall.

▸ Locals call the Goodwill in southeast Portland "the Bins." Unlike other Goodwill shops where the products are organized and shelved, the Bins is just that—bin after bin of stuff that you literally have to pick through. Shannon frequents this Goodwill often and during one outing found a collection of old blue bottles, which are now displayed on her living room window trim. The log pieces, which together make for a unique and clever coffee table, were made from a large holly bush that had to be cut down to make room for the new home. The 1940s three-piece sectional couch was found at a neighbor's estate sale; Shannon had it reupholstered in gray fabric and burlap she found at the Bins. The painting (framed in scrap wood) and the stacked box and suitcases are also all objects she found along the way.

▸▸ The living room is a proverbial salvage feast. Reclaimed brick surrounds a new energy-efficient gas fireplace. The gorgeous mantel and surround are made from wood that once was the original bungalow's sun porch. The freestanding white column was found at a garage sale and the chairs and couches are all estate-sale finds that Shannon had recovered in dual fabrics including used coffee-bean sacks. The painting was a housewarming gift from a friend (who found it at Goodwill) and the rest of the salvage details were garage-sale finds.

When Shannon and Glenn's son, Chase, has friends stay overnight, they are comfortable in these twin beds in the guestroom. The bed frames were repurposed from Chase's bunk bed. The light fixture was converted from an old heater lamp by Old Portland Architectural and Hardware. Chase's paintings are framed above the beds, and most of the bedding, including the old football "pillows," were found at garage sales. The narrow vintage table between the beds serves as a nightstand and divider as well as a decorative piece.

Shannon's home project has become known as the REX Project—Reuse Everything eXperiment. A project this ambitious is not for the faint of heart, but Shannon proved it could be done—with a little ingenuity and *lot* of community support, including from all the building professionals she worked with. And in the end, she managed to not only save money but also create a gorgeous design.

If everyone embarking on a building or remodeling project were to use even just one or two of Shannon's ideas, we'd be that much closer to dumpster-free construction—a lofty goal, perhaps, but one well worth pursuing.

The exterior fireplace, also made with reclaimed bricks, backs up against the indoor fireplace in the living room. The shiplap siding on the entire west side of the house was the original bungalow's siding. To preserve the history of the first home, Shannon didn't have the old nail holes filled when the siding was painted. The mix-and-match vintage chairs, pottery, candelabra, and frames above the mantel are all garage-sale finds. This exterior living space is a fun place to hang out and listen to passersby comment to each other about how the house was built without using a single dumpster. The whole neighborhood takes pride in the house and what Shannon and her family accomplished.

The master bedroom is kept simple with an old marble-and-metal base at the end of the bed. Above the vintage metal bed frame is a piece of a very old green fireplace mantel. It was already cut to that size and perfect for displaying shells and other seashore finds. The extra-large white cabinet, made entirely of heart pine, was in the shed of a nearby house that was being torn down. It now serves as a wardrobe.

Jane removed the outdated upper cabinets and added simple base cabinet boxes and used vintage shutters (cut in half) as the doors. Because she liked the original color on the shutters, she had the box painted to match. She then found an old window frame and had mirrored glass added to it. The countertop and backsplash tiles were salvaged from another job.

HAPPY COLORS

Tybee Island, Georgia

Jane Coslick is well known for her interior design and restoration work, especially around the Tybee Island and Savannah, Georgia, area. She's saved many old cottages from demolition, and when they couldn't be saved, she salvaged as much of their material as possible to use on other projects. Jane's signature look is built on salvaged materials and sunny, bright colors.

When Jane found a rundown 1946 cottage filled with hollow-core doors and dark rough-hewn wood walls, many of her friends tried to discourage her from buying it, thinking it needed too much work. Indeed, it had languished on the market for 6 years before Jane purchased it. But Jane could see past all the outdated pieces and, sure enough, she was able to transform it into a light, airy beach cottage. She owned it for many years and recently sold it to a friend, totally furnished and move-in ready.

One of Jane's trademarks is slipcovering second-hand furnishings. Easy to clean, slipcovers give a room a welcoming, casual look while keeping the style simple and crisp. Jane finds the furniture she slipcovers at a variety of places including Habitat for Humanity, garage sales, and the homes of friends who are updating their rooms. The shape, size, and sturdiness of the piece are important, but most essential is the comfort. And, of course, it has to be easy to slipcover (not all furniture is). Jane has the slipcovers made professionally for a great look that will last over time.

Jane picks up many of her antiques from John Beuter, a collector and antiques dealer, including this Egyptian wrought-iron gate that serves as a headboard. Attached directly to the wall, it gives the illusion of a large bed frame without taking up the valuable space that a frame sometimes does. A second-hand table functions as a nightstand, and a curtain hung on the old salvaged door (left with its original patina and knob) gives the room some privacy while still allowing light to filter in from the kitchen.

The shed in the backyard was transformed into what Jane calls an "inspiration room"—a place to go to relax and get inspired. It's also great as an extra guestroom. The custom-sized beds, made out of wood from old docks, were fabricated by Charlie Elis, a local builder. The chandelier was found sitting inside a fireplace at a construction site. Jane took it out, cleaned it up, and repaired it, and it now glows beautifully in this tiny space.

▲ Jane repurposed an old spice cabinet from the kitchen for the medicine cabinet over the toilet, and she painted the frame of the vintage mirror a bright orange to complement the blue walls and zebra shower curtain.

◀ What was once a laundry closet is now a cozy retreat and extra bedroom. Tucked between the salvaged bi-fold doors is a bed covered with bright pillows and accessories. Instead of removing the old floorboards, Jane painted them an ocean blue color. The second-hand chair in the front room was slipcovered in the same style as the ones throughout the rest of the house. A salvaged box works well as a side table.

◀◀ Created entirely from salvaged material, this romantic gazebo is what dreams are made of. The windows hanging from the ceiling were traded with a builder for other material, and the gingerbread boards and posts are from an old Victorian home in Savannah. The rest of the salvaged pieces were painted white to match. The vintage chaise lounge was a gift from one of Jane's clients, and the old table and other accessories are all salvaged or second-hand pieces Jane found along the way.

▲ Giving the space a sense of continuity, reclaimed Indonesian hardwood from old shipping pallets was used as wainscoting here. Its various uses in the home show just how versatile and beautiful scrap pallet wood can be. Leftover piping was used to create a footrest for the bar that butts up to the kitchen.

▶ Kerri's love of Asian style shows in the family room, where an old Chinese screen backed with fabric and hung with Krown Lab barn-door hardware not only makes for a stunning wall display but also hides the television when it is not in use. The chaise lounge, which Kerri's parents found at an auction and she re-covered with a blue fabric, a vintage blue metal cart, and a table made from an old spruce tree by a neighbor, create a homey feel in this room.

"A TRAVELER'S TOUCH"

Portland, Oregon

Traveling to far-flung locations around the globe is one of Kerri Hoyt-Pack's passions—matched only by her passion for bringing the styles and pieces she discovers back home to Portland. With the help of designer Anne De Wolf of Arciform Design Build, Kerri completed a gorgeous remodel with a refreshing French-Asian chic edge. The house showcases the unique qualities of salvage and is a place Kerri and her family will enjoy for years to come.

The shelving in Kerri Hoyt-Pack's kitchen was custom-made by Arciform out of the reclaimed Indonesian hardwood, picked up at Port of Portland. The frames were welded together and then the pieces of wood were planed and glued for the shelves. They have an "industrial country" look, which works well with the beadboard ceiling and Florence Broadhurst wallpaper. The two moveable islands were designed by Anne De Wolf of Aciform, using the same materials as those for the open shelving. Their zinc tops are great for doing prep work and are easily cleaned. Kerri found the vintage sink through an online source.

With the custom-made salvaged shelving, mentioned earlier, lots of white subway tiles, and Kerri's collection of antique and vintage pieces, this kitchen exudes a French country look. Kerri loves collecting and remembers were she got every piece—from a business trip in Amsterdam (the blue bread box) to a garage sale at the home of a breadmaker (the blue bread bowl). Vintage clocks, baskets, stools, jars, signs—all fit nicely in her open shelving scheme. Mixing a vintage butcher-block table with a marble-topped table with black metal machinist legs (perfect for rolling dough) works well in a kitchen that has no customary cabinetry.

◂ Kerri's daughter's upstairs bathroom has a totally different look. With its pink walls and large prints, oversized dresser and mirror, and vintage cake dish and props, it makes you feel like you're peeking into the window of a dollhouse.

▾ The downstairs bathroom uses a vintage dresser, not as a vanity but rather for storage. A coat of high-gloss white paint helps keep it water-resistant. The vintage claw-foot tub was from a friend who was getting rid of it. With its elevated height and bright blue base, the tub feels like it holds a place of honor in this quaint, country-bistro-feeling bathroom. The wall shelving was made from old shutters, cut down to a smaller size and placed atop old metal brackets. The vintage chandelier and curtains add a dramatic flair.

◂ Using old screen doors, beadboard, and a little ingenuity, Kerri and her husband, Dan, transformed this guestroom into a multipurpose guestroom/office space for Kerri. Dan constructed these built-in closets on either side of Kerri's desk, creating a nook for her office space. The desk itself was once an old door, now fitted with a layer of glass.

The dining-room table, an heirloom from Kerri's husband's family, is surrounded by more of her finds, including the Indian wedding chairs with worn blue patina and the two second-hand wicker patio chairs she sprayed to match. The runner is a vintage linen grain sack that Kerri bought on eBay. Mixed with antique pieces she has found around the world, including many in Shanghai, these salvaged pieces speak volumes about traditions in different corners of the globe.

Once part of the driveway, the outside patio area of Michelle de la Vega's converted garage is now an oasis of second-hand containers filled with plants and trees. Michelle picked up the patio table at a yard sale and got the chairs from a car mechanic's shop where she happened to be getting new tires for her truck. A pallet serves as the porch to step inside the house. With lots of added windows (for the loft area) and full glass doors the small garage is now filled with light. The artwork on the back wall is her own and the coffee table, which she fabricated herself, is made from salvaged mahogany and steel.

GARAGE MOD

Seattle, Washington

Like many studio-apartment dwellers in big cities, Michelle de la Vega lives in 250 square feet. But this isn't an apartment in a metropolis—it's a repurposed garage in a Seattle neighborhood. Michelle—an artist, welder, and interior designer—decided to transform her garage into a living space so that she could rent out her house for additional income. Her spectacular renovation shows that living small can be done with big style.

Michelle made use of her welding skills for the bathroom, creating the countertop for the sink to sit on out of salvaged metal. The hooks, old industrial latches she found at Habitat for Humanity, were welded on flanges to attach them to the wall. Michelle picked up the tub at Second Use and stripped and painted the base a steel gray. She replaced the tub feet with a salvaged-wood base that she made with her father, but she kept the old feet for decor in the space. The vintage Thonet chair functions as a table as well as a place to sit down. The artwork is hers, made from salvaged tin shingles.

By stroke of luck, a woodstove was already sitting in the garage when Michelle bought it, although it wasn't in use or attached. Michelle hooked it up and lined the wall and floor around it with salvaged bricks. Along with a small gas furnace, it serves as the heat source for the garage home. The sleeping loft, built out of salvaged beams, is reached by an industrial ladder salvaged from an old ship. Because of the limited space, Michelle cleverly used old lockers that United Airlines was giving away for her clothing and vintage trunks for additional storage. The vintage George Mulhauser Plycraft chair, which she found on Craigslist and restored herself, is in the perfect spot to see the garden space outside.

The kitchen area is simple and cozy. Small but deep, the salvaged industrial mop sink works perfectly in the space. The two metal canisters that serve as recycling and trash were picked up from a United Airlines employee locker room. The old barn light above the sink was a gift from a Mercedes mechanic whose shop was next door to Michelle's art studio; she rewired and installed it. The stainless steel countertop is a second-hand restaurant counter, and old wine boxes are used as the drawers underneath. Everything Michelle needs is right at her fingertips.

Kim Clements and Joe Schneider's dining room is a fun place to hang out, and with a custom dining table top made from an old bowling-alley lane and a wall covered with an old school blackboard framed in scrap mahogany pieces, you can't help but assume it's a lively one, too. The chairs are a mix of new (Carl Hansen Wishbone chairs) and vintage finds (like the green chair at the end of the table, which Kim found at a local antique mall). The pull-down world map (ordered online from Amazon) and old dictionary sit on a vintage red stand and are ready the moment you want to take a break from eating and learn a thing or two. With the colors of the map pulling it all together, it's a happy, welcoming dining space.

The kitchen also incorporates some nice vintage details—lamps, ceiling pendant, clock, and a white enameled vintage stove, not to mention all the dishware and decor.

THE MIX AND MATCH

Seattle, Washington

Kim Clements and Joe Schneider have a busy life, between their kids, pets, and job as owners of J.A.S. Design Build. They're in and out of their home often, but that didn't stop them from making it a happy environment through a remodel that included many salvage finds. With an open plan in mind they created structured space using unique materials and high standards. A dining room wall with a salvaged blackboard, a vintage stove, recycled lighting components, quality reupholstered furnishings, and custom made stained glass windows are just a few of the pieces throughout this bungalow style home in a northern suburb of Seattle. The importance of usability and liveability, as well as a commitment to materials that will stand the test of time, are key to how Kim and Joe planned their remodel and how they run their company.

In the living room are stained glass windows (sometimes called "magic lanterns") that have vintage glass projection images. Kim designed the windows after prayer rug designs and had the vintage slides set in the middle of them. A vintage dining table that Kim found on Craigslist was cut down and painted brown to make a spacious coffee table perfect for games, including those that make use of Kim's dice collection. The old orange metal machinist box was picked up at a Boeing surplus sale. If you look closely, you'll see that the brass base of the table lamp is made from a large shell casing from World War II. Kim is an eclectic collector, always on the lookout for everything from vintage jewelry to old yardsticks, which she displays like flower arrangements.

Off of the living room is a tiny library alcove, which you enter through custom-made salvaged mahogany doors with punched and galvanized sheet metal. Collections of building blocks and vintage industrial boxes not only add a bright burst of color but also store extra toys and pictures. Stylish in a chic-eclectic way, the vintage Chinese basket that sits near the couch is filled with blocks and vintage trucks, ready for a play date.

▲ The south-facing sitting area off of the dining room enjoys a lot of light, which is welcome in this Seattle home. Kim found the two matching solid 1980s chairs at a garage sale—she gave them new down cushions and had them re-covered in a seersucker fabric. Tucked into a corner, on top of a 1930s Iranian rug, the low Japanese tea table that Kim picked up at an antique shop fits perfectly in the space. She liked it because it was lower than a regular coffee table.

▶ Sitting on the built-in behind the bed is another of Kim's collections—hand molds for latex gloves. The green machinist table lamp, picked up from a local vintage industrial dealer, was rewired and attached to the wall. It can be adjusted to reach over the bed, great for night reading. The elephant, a Goodwill find, stands guard on the bed. On every bedroom door in the house is a vintage mailbox, in which family members leave one another nice notes—a clever and personal use of vintage pieces. Kim found the mailboxes on eBay. The bird, a cement garden ornament she found at an antique shop, now holds her door open.

Making use of the gable end of the house, Kim and Joe added a rod and curtains to create a closet space. A vintage dress form holds Kim's mix of old and new jewelry—a clever alternative to a jewelry box, and one that turns the pieces into a decor element when Kim isn't wearing them. An old stool and antique rug and hooks complete the space.

Vintage ceiling light fixtures—most found online—appear in every room of the house. Kim wanted to keep the remodeling costs down, and vintage porcelain fixtures came to mind not only because they're affordable but also because they fit with the style of the home. They left the shades off several of them, letting the details of the wood ceiling, the fixture itself, and the white-tipped bulb stand out. The color scheme of the room comes from the bright-orange salvaged stool found at an antique mall. The bathroom door is also salvaged—they removed the wood panel at the top of the door and added glass to allow natural light to flow through the room into the dark hallway beside it.

The open floor plan of Susan and Ryan Hayes's living and dining room allows the dining table and chairs to be the show-stopping pieces in the space. Just as in an old farmhouse, the functional piece is also the main decor. The table is made by Five Corners Antiques in Essex Junction, a local antique dealer who also builds farmhouse tables with salvaged boards, legs, and skirts. Susan collected the mismatched antique chairs over time. The back wall, painted with chalkboard paint, makes the table and chairs really stand out, and together, all the textures, colors, and patina combine for a feeling of pleasant nostalgia. The banister railing and post were salvaged from an old farmhouse in northern Vermont.

Susan and Ryan wanted unique touches, like these sinks found at Mason Brothers Architectural Salvage Shop. Once in Middlebury College dormitories, they were outfitted with new faucets and plumbing and now serve as his-and-hers basins in the master bathroom. The side table is made with a salvaged tree slab and a vintage office chair base.

As old farming families did, Susan and Ryan embrace the attractiveness of functionality. Vintage country-store candy jars, Ball canning jars, and locally made pottery are displayed on the open shelving in the kitchen. Canning jars can easily be found at recycle centers and second-hand shops; old country-store candy jars are more often found at antique shops or online.

SMALL FARM, BIG IDEAS

Champlain Valley Area, Vermont

It all started with an inspiration—to build a simple, efficient home on a beautiful piece of land that reminded Susan and Ryan Hayes of Ryan's grandparents' farm. Using local resources, recycled and salvaged goods, and energy-efficient products, they did just that—with a flair that shows that environmentally low-impact design doesn't preclude style. Salvaged pieces that are warm and welcoming are combined with simple, clean lines to create a home that feels contemporary yet harkens to the past.

Stopping at "free" signs along country roads led to some great finds, such as the old apple crates here, which serve as nightstands and are filled with books about farming, knitting, and parenting. Susan and Ryan found the blue dresser at an antique shop, Slate Barn Antiques, a few miles from their home. The bedding is a mixture of new and vintage quilts and throws.

In keeping with the clean lines and simple spaces throughout the rest of the house, the kitchen is a mix of modern and utilitarian, ready for baskets of fruit and vegetables to come in from the garden to be canned. The countertop is a product called PaperStone, which is made from 100% post-consumer recycled paper and petroleum-free resins. It has the strength of steel but looks more like stone and is an easy surface to clean. The movable island of metal and wood (made by Boos Block) keeps the space looking open and is easy to work around. Many of Susan's bowls and mason jars are recycled; she uses them both as glasses and for storage.

The cozy entrance to Jason's home is just big enough for the three attached red metal chairs that he found at a Pier Antique Show in New York City—they were once part of the stands at a Texas rodeo. The old metal gear-wheel table (the plant stand at left) with a reclaimed wood top was made by Andy Whitcomb, who creates industrial-style furniture pieces out of reclaimed materials. A vintage gnome that Jason found at a flea market in Park Slope, Brooklyn, is the official greeter.

A FLAIR FOR FURNISHINGS

Seattle, Washington

Jason Mathews has always been a visual storyteller, even when he lived in New York City and worked as a segment producer for a well-known morning show. Now, relocated to Seattle with his family, he's pursued another path as an interior designer and shop owner of Sheridan + Company. Because Jason is always on the lookout for great design, he gets to meet some talented artisans who work with unusual material—scrap metal to vintage tennis rackets—to create one of a kind pieces. Jason loves all styles and is not afraid to put them together. Garage sale finds, flea market discoveries, collectable bowls and accessories, one-of-a-kind artisan made designs, Craiglist scores, popular mid-century style furnishings and New England antique pieces can be found throughout Jason's home.

▲ Jason and his family love hanging out on the back deck, especially on sunny Seattle days. He bought the old green wicker chairs at Pacific Antique Gallery in Seattle.

◀ Jason started putting this guestroom together with a search on Craigslist, where he found these matching twin wood beds, which he brought home and painted black. His next discovery, at an antique shop, was the old barn light, which he had rewired for residential (rather than industrial) use. The dresser, also painted black, was found at the Fremont Sunday Street Market, a well-known flea market in the Seattle area. The pheasant atop the dresser, bought at an estate sale, reminds Jason of his childhood home in Idaho. The base of the custom-made nightstand was once a piece of brick-making machinery, and the top is a piece of salvaged wood. The lamp was made from what are called the "knees" of an old cypress tree. Filled with salvaged finds, this cozy bedroom is ready for guests to arrive at a moment's notice.

Jason sells many of Andy Whitcomb's salvaged furniture pieces in his shop, Sheridan + Company, but many also end up in his own home, like this farmhouse-style table. Jason's collection of white pottery is mostly McCoy, a brand produced in the United States between the late 1800s and early 1900s.

Midcentury modern pieces, a style Jason is very fond of, are throughout the house. The coffee table was bought on eBay and Jason found the Atomic-style light fixture at a Consign by Design store in Seattle. Overseen by a portrait of a woman they call "the pretty lady," are vintage chairs that Jason bought at a Seattle shop called Re-Soul. The floor lamp is also vintage, as is the wooden side table at the end of the room.

HOW THE WEST IS WON

Phoenix, Arizona

Annie Haviland, the homeowner of this Southwestern ranch, although trained as an architectural draftsperson, didn't take a "straight line" approach with her interior design, going instead for a blur of Western, Spanish, eclectic, and feminine elements. The layering of textures, materials, and styles gives the home a comfortable, lived-in look—perfect for a family who owns a horse business and often comes home dusty from the corrals. To get a style just right for ranch living, Annie called on friends and family members Shayce Igleski, Lettie Peterson, and Susan Haviland, who not only gave her design advice but also were partners in crime when it came to shopping for great salvage and vintage finds. With a natural eye for styling, Annie pulled together ideas she'd seen in books, magazines, and at some of her favorite vintage shops, layering different pieces to give each room its own personality and style.

Annie Haviland added some feminine details to soften the strong stone and granite kitchen in her Arizona home. She found all the trays, plates, vases, silver pieces, and even the birdcage at various vintage and antique shops in and around the Phoenix area. The display on the island, with the vintage scale and platters, is similar to one she saw at Sweet Salvage, one of her favorite shopping spots (see p. 155).

The boys' room is all about fun! These little cowboys get to sleep on beds set atop salvaged pallets on wheels. With a handy and helpful husband, Annie was able to make these fun beds for the boys, including the headboards made with salvaged coffee bags. The light fixture on the left is an ingenious use of an old galvanized bucket picked up at Sweet Salvage. The other light is even more creative—Annie bought a piece of driftwood at a floral supply store and wrapped it with holiday lights. The dresser, metal boxes, and crate were found at a variety of salvage locations, and the entire wall is lined with chicken wire, which lets the boys hang stuff on the walls without making any holes.

This wall-papering project between the bedroom and bathroom took some time to complete. Annie found three different sizes of old books at Goodwill, ripped out the pages, decoupaged them, and then glazed them on the wall, giving it a rustic, worldly look. Through the doorway, the vintage cast-iron claw-foot tub, found on Craigslist, takes center stage. Annie had a company that specializes in sandblasting come to the house to sandblast the sides of the tub, which she then painted with a blue metallic paint. The vintage chandelier above the tub was picked up at a second-hand store and repainted, and the panels on the wall were from a friend who was getting rid of them—Annie added fabric inside them for a softer look. Next to the tub is a three-layered table filled with vintage trinkets and bath accessories. The marble bust, from a vintage shop, adds another feminine touch to the space.

▲ On cool evenings the family spends a lot of time on the garden patio, which includes an eating area, and Annie has made it a romantic and inviting place to be with an old table, mismatched salvaged chairs, and lights with shades covered in layers of lace and fabric.

▸▸ Annie considers herself lucky to have a husband who raises an eyebrow only once in a while when she's putting together vignettes filled with salvaged couches, tables, trunks, and chairs. Painted a bright blue, the old brass chandelier in this mix-and-match corner pulls everything together, making it a perfect casual gathering spot or reading nook. Creatively displayed on the table inside an old frame are some more vintage finds, some from Poppy's Home Decor in Mesa, Arizona.

▲ The master bedroom adds a little luxury to the Western look. Layers of vintage trunks, frames, and even Annie's husband's cowboy boots blend beautifully with the elegant black-framed bed. The vintage chandelier provides a nice, soft glow for night reading. The large trunks make a strong statement and help balance the oversized bed, which would dwarf a smaller nightstand.

◀ The kids' bathroom is filled with unique finds. Annie gave the shower curtain an extra flair by adding ruffles at the bottom and raising the whole bar up to the high ceiling, making the room seem extra tall. The vintage chandelier, found at a shabby chic antique shop, reflects beautifully in the vintage mirror. Old shelves and brackets above the toilet display a variety of small salvage finds.

Annie used layering to a very different effect in her daughter's room. Inspired by various looks—one she saw in an Anthropologie catalogue and another at Sweet Salvage (see p. 155)—she painted the back wall black and pinned vintage lace tablecloths to it. Against that backdrop is a vintage pink headboard she got from a friend and little green second-hand table she found at a Phoenix shop called Rust and Rose. The old light fixtures were rewired and strips of salvaged fabric were used to hide the chains. Soft but powerful, this room is perfect for any cowgirl.

Before they could move in, Jessica Helgerson and Yianni Doulis needed to winterize this former shipyard worker's cottage. Jessica and Yianni used shiplapped Douglas fir from one of the barns on the property. (The wood had originally been salvaged from a grain building south of Portland.) The couple painted the wood white on the ceiling and side walls but left it natural on the back wall for a stunning visual contrast. Yianni made the dining table himself from local salvaged walnut and found the mismatched vintage Paul McCobb chairs through Craigslist and antique dealers. The vintage stove was also found on Craigslist. Its hood is covered in the same salvaged wood as that on the wall, allowing it to almost disappear visually. A single shelf holds flour and grains in vintage blue Ball jars, and a second-hand metal drawer serves as a breadbox. The woodstove keeps the family cozy during evening meals.

SALVAGE SIMPLICITY

Sauvie Island, Oregon

It's hard to believe that this gorgeous cottage on an island near Portland, Oregon, was first built to house shipyard workers in the 1940s. What's even more astounding is that it subsequently floated down a river during a flood, eventually ending up in a spot downstream where it became a goose-checking station. By the time interior designer Jessica Helgerson and her husband, architect Yianni Doulis, happened upon it, it had moved into its third incarnation—as a summer cottage rental property. With great vision and a love of the surrounding property, which included barns and lots of land, Jessica and Yianni decided to renovate the tiny, 540-square-foot cottage, repurposing it once more and calling it home.

The same salvaged wood was used for the built-in couch and bookcases. All the wood was cleaned, sanded, and painted in Benjamin Moore "White Opulence" for a clean look. The vintage cabinet holds the family's dishware collection and vintage pottery. Surrounded by books on gardening, growing fruit trees, and cheese-making (Yianni is also a cheese-maker), the family spends a lot of quality time relaxing in the living room.

Reclaimed wood is the cottage's centerpiece, and they displayed it creatively in various forms, from its natural state as an accent wall in the kitchen, to pieces they painted and layered along the wall in a shiplap pattern. This cottage is an extraordinary example of how one salvaged wood source can produce multiple styles and functions depending on where it's used—on walls, ceilings, floors, built-ins, cabinets, drawers, paneling, and shelving. Reduce, reuse, and recycle are part of the couple's mantra in their work as a designer and architect, and this beautifully remodeled cottage shows that they practice what they preach.

◂ This crisp bathroom feels spa-like in its design, with natural light bouncing off the white walls. The tub was salvaged from a friend's demolition project and the vintage sink was original to the house. A piece of recycled mirror that extends to the ceiling reflects all the salvaged wood paneling in the space. The serene, simple aesthetic of this design is what makes it so inviting.

▸▸ Again keeping the design simple, Jessica and Yianni carried the paneling into the children's room, creating a built-in bunk bed and pull-out closet space. The built-ins leave plenty of space in the room for the kids to play—when they're not out roaming the acres of gardens on the property.

Repurposing the 1938 warehouse building that housed the Hancock family lumber business began with the help of a local church youth group. As a fundraiser, they removed all the nails, bolts, split rings, and hardware from the deconstructed warehouse lumber. It took 6 weeks and over 9 acres to sort everything from the building, including 12x12, 10x10, and 8x8 timbers, and 1x6 boards of exceptional fine-grain Douglas fir. The wood was used in various ways throughout the Hancock family's new home. Here, it was re-sawn and planed for the stair treads, flooring, and kitchen cabinetry. The stair handrail post was one of the 10x10 beams, cut to size and capped with a vintage Japanese glass float found on the beach by one of the workers during construction. The trim work, window frames, and arched truss-bow window-header pieces were left rough, showing their original circular-sawn textures. All the reclaimed lumber was finished with Aqua Zar water-based polyurethane antique finish.

The barn-board wall was once the exterior siding of the warehouse. A good cleaning with a brush sander exposed the natural texture and color of the rough-sawn wood. The wall was coated with the same non-yellowing polyurethane to maintain the natural reclaimed look. The wood on the floor is the same as that on the walls—the amazing difference in color was achieved by re-milling and planing it, which shaved off the old patina. The custom kitchen cabinetry, made of the same reclaimed wood, was built by Craig Spooner of Western Cabinets. With joists and a huge beam running through the entire space, the lodge-style ceiling reflects the history of the warehouse. To allow the salvaged wood roof joists to be seen, the design team installed rigid foam board insulation on top of the structural sheathing.

Beautiful details like the window trim retain the nicks of the old factory materials, bringing a legacy of sustainability into the Hancock family's future. The metal railing system along the loft and stairwell—as well as the towel bars, coat hooks, toiler-paper holders, and cabinet pulls elsewhere in the house—is made from the old washers, brackets, screws, bolts, and split rings that were pulled out of the wood after the warehouse was dismantled.

A RECLAIMED LEGACY

The Oregon Coast

"An adventure in deconstruction and partnership with a village of craftsmen" is what Terry Hancock called it. When he and his father, Gary, closed their family lumber business in 1993, they deconstructed the large truss bow warehouse and used the materials to build a new oceanside home along the Oregon coast. The goal was to connect the family's past to the present and future generations through their new home. With the help of architect Nathan Good and his small team, they created a LEED Gold home that not only stand ups to Oregon's wet coastal weather but also brings the warmth of the family's own reclaimed wood into every aspect of the design.

▲ This sink was found at a reclaimed wood business called Wood is Wonderful. The hardware throughout the kitchen (and the rest of the house) was custom designed by the Hancocks, using more metal salvaged from the warehouse, including old bolts, washers, and nuts. It was finished with a copper vein powder coat finish.

▶ This vintage 1910 hotel sink from Rejuvenation still had its original faucets intact. The Douglas fir from the warehouse was used in a few different ways throughout the bathroom—planed for the cabinets, with its curved edge for the backsplash, uniquely cut window trim, and rough-hewn on the ceiling, with joists left exposed. The vintage lights above the sink were set right into the full wall mirror.

▸ More of the wood was used in the bedrooms, including for barn doors hung on sliders to separate the sleeping space from the bathroom and closet. The structural beams along the wall (from the 12x12 beams of the warehouse) were left partially exposed, adding to the lodge feeling of the house.

▾ In some ways, just this simple cutout circle on a handrail—left over from a bolt that was once embedded in the wood—tells the whole story of this remarkable home. It stands as both a mark of the family's past and a symbol of its future. On the grandest of scales, the Hancocks show us how to travel this path of renewal elegantly.

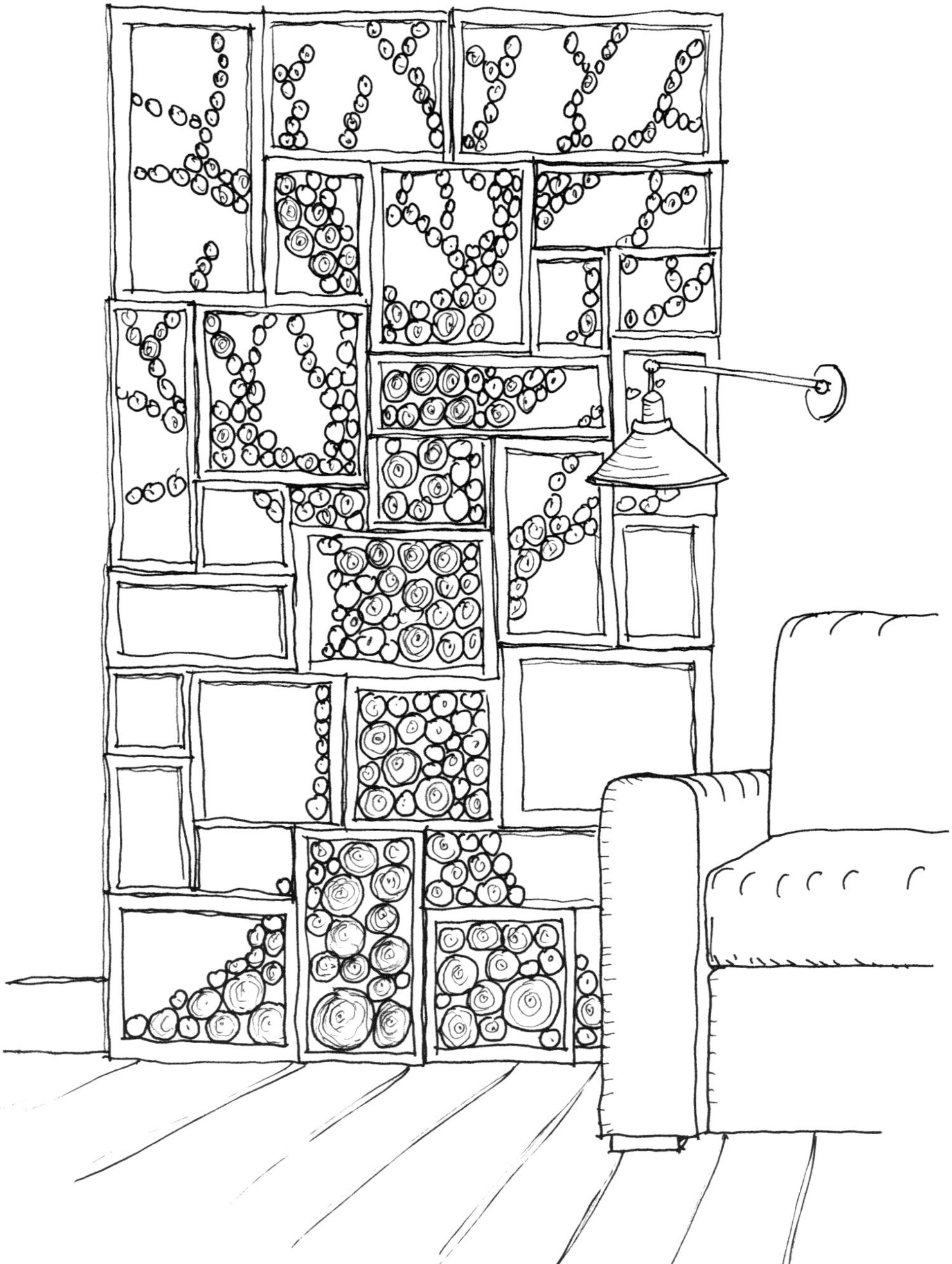

◂◂ When considering a do-it-yourself project, think about how to put recycled materials to use in a new way. Old frames can be found everywhere—instead of hanging just one, create a full-wall masterpiece by painting several the same color and inserting slivers of cut tree branch ends (or whatever you'd like) inside the frame. A simple and stunning do-it-yourself talking piece!

Do-It-Yourself Projects

As with anything, the more you practice the more comfortable you'll become with do-it-yourself salvage projects. It may take some time to figure out whether your first recycled chandelier needs to be rewired—not to mention how you want to change it aesthetically—but the next chandelier will be easier and by the third you may feel confident enough to do the rewiring yourself. And even if you aren't, hundreds of vintage-light specialty shops exist, along with artisans who can do that part for you. Regardless of the type of salvage you're using—and how comfortable you are working with it—experts like these will be an important part of your resource list.

I have created nearly two hundred do-it-yourself projects for the DIY NETWORK online, including eight videos, all made from recycled, second-hand, and salvaged material, and several dozen more for clients, family, and friends. Creating something new out of something old never gets boring. The salvage endeavors detailed here will give you a taste of the variety of easy projects you can try your hand at—coffee tables, curtains, headboards, chairs, lights, lamps, home decor, gifts, and more.

Sometimes I begin by conceptualizing the final product first and then hunting down just the right materials. Other times I happen upon the salvaged materials and let *them* inspire what the project will be. Whichever approach you take, doing it yourself can be lots of fun.

CHICKEN-COOP COFFEE TABLE

It's easy to put a coffee table together with an old wooden chicken coop or something similar, like a wooden box or a flat, hard suitcase. These items can be found in a variety of locations—garage sales, your local antique shop or recycle store, and of course online. The piece of glass for this table was from another table I found at Goodwill and used in a different location. If you find a piece at a recycle shop for only a few dollars, it's well worth getting. (Remember, though, that the glass must be "tempered"—made so that it won't have sharp edges if it breaks. You can have your local glass shop cut it to size.)

Materials

Wooden chicken coop or box
Drill
Wire cutters
Pliers
White paint (or spray paint)
4 coffee table legs at hardware store
(with flat bases and screw-in brackets)
Steel brush
Scrub brush
1/4 cup of bleach
Bowl for water
Hot glue gun and glue sticks
Tempered glass top (optional)

Step 1. If there is wire on your chicken coop, just cut it off and use pliers to pull out the staples.

Step 2. Scrub the coop with a steel brush and then wash it down well. I took this coop outside and hosed it down. After it dried completely, I scrubbed it again with a 1/4 bleach, 3/4 water solution. When you work with old wood, it's important to get it as clean as possible—this gets rid of not only all the dirt but also any critters that might be hanging around. Let it dry completely—at least a day or two.

Step 3. Once the coop is completely dry, turn it upside down and mark the four corners where you will be putting the legs. Start the corner at 3 inches from the outside (on both sides).

Step 4. Place the bracket on the corner mark and use the drill to screw it into place. Make sure the bracket has the correct side up before you screw it in.

Step 5. With the bracket securely in place, screw in the leg. Make sure the leg goes in straight, and keep turning it until it's tight.

Step 6. Painting is the last step. Whenever possible, I use recycled paint from a rebuild center, but because this coop had so many thin spindles and it was impossible to reach inside, I used white spray paint. You can use semi-gloss or gloss—whichever effect you like best. Cover all sides, including the inside. Let it dry and then add a second coat. Before adding the glass top, I put drops of hot glue on the top of the table at the corners to keep the glass from sliding around.

LAYERED, PAINTED FRAMES

Layering old frames is one of the easiest ways to decorate any room. You've probably browsed framed prints at antique or second-hand shops, passing over the prints you didn't like. But how many times have you noticed the frames? It's easy to miss gorgeous, handcrafted frames when we focus only on the art inside them. Good frames can be found at antique fairs—with nothing in them—or sometimes at Goodwill with a bad poster stuck inside. I've also found them at furniture recycle centers, flea markets, and garage sales. Depending on their size, their ornamentation, and who's selling them, they can range in price from around $5 to $100. (And don't worry about mismatched colors—a little paint quickly cures that.)

Old frames are very versatile when it comes to achieving the particular style you want. Going for a cottage look? Try covering an entire living room wall with frames painted white, and put a large seashell painted bright blue in the middle of each. Looking for something more modern? Push a bunch of frames

together, so their outside edges touch. Then paint them black and add a letter in the middle of each—for instance, a vintage industrial metal letter from an old factory. For a kid's room, layer the frames again, using a different color for each, and in the middle put the footprint they gave you at the hospital—a perfect way to display a tiny memento from your baby's first day.

Materials

3 to 5 frames that allow for 1 to 2 inches in between them
1 small frame with print or mirror (optional)
Picture-frame hooks (depending on the weight of the frame)
Paintbrush
Paint (sample size)

Step 1. Pick out a bunch of frames of different shapes and sizes. Make sure they're in good condition and that the corners are secure and tight.

Step 2. Lay the frames on the floor and see how they fit inside each other. If one frame is almost touching another, it's not a good choice.

Step 3. Decide whether you want to leave the frames as they already are, or if you'd rather paint them, decoupage them, or strip them down to their natural wood.

Step 4. If you decide to repaint them, start by lightly sanding the frame, wiping it clean, and then applying the paint. You can use a solid finish or leave a little of the frame underneath showing through. Let dry and, if necessary, paint a second coat. Hang each frame separately using picture-frame hooks—rather than wire, which may show through the layers—placed flat against the back of each frame.

QUICK-FIX CHAIR COVER

Professional slipcovering or reupholstering can change the entire look of an heirloom piece—not to mention extend its lifespan for another hundred years or so. But when you're in a rush, this quick-fix method works well as a temporary solution, buying you some time before you get the job done right by a professional in the upholstery field.

Materials

Second-hand upholstered chair with upholstery tacks
5 to 10 yards of fabric (sometimes I use old blankets, bedspreads, or even painter's tarps)
Needle and thread (same color as fabric)
2 cans of adhesive spray (my favorite is Elmer's multi-purpose adhesive spray)
Upholstery nail heads (found at hardware store)

Pliers
Flathead screwdriver
Hammer
Scissors
3 to 4 drop cloths

Step 1. Clean the chair well. I usually air it out, then spray it with a bleach/water solution (1/4 bleach, 3/4 water), let it dry, and then vacuum it. Make sure the chair is completely clean before you start the project.

Step 2. Use the flathead screwdriver and pliers to remove the upholstery tacks—I do one side at a time. (You'll replace them with new ones.)

Step 3. Cut pieces of fabric to fit along the chair, making sure to give yourself plenty of extra fabric to work with (you can always cut the excess off).

Step 4. Spray the part of the chair you're working on with the adhesive, and place the new fabric down on it, pressing and smoothing it to take out any folds or kinks. The spray is forgiving, so if you need to adjust the position of the fabric, just pull it up and then press it back down. Make sure you tuck plenty of extra fabric into the seams—otherwise it will pull out when you sit in the chair, and the old fabric will show.

Step 5. Start at the bottom front of the chair, then work to the arms, and finish with the back. When you get to the edges, fold the fabric under to give it a finished edge. Also, make sure to cover the finished areas with a drop cloth so they don't get sticky from the spray adhesive.

Step 6. Use the upholstery nail heads on the parts of the chair where they can be nailed into the wood. On some chairs this part will be on the arms; on others it will be on the back or base.

Step 7. Fold any extra fabric underneath the chair and glue it to the bottom with a hot glue gun. If there are places where the fabric needs to be attached but where you can't use the nail heads, use the needle and thread.

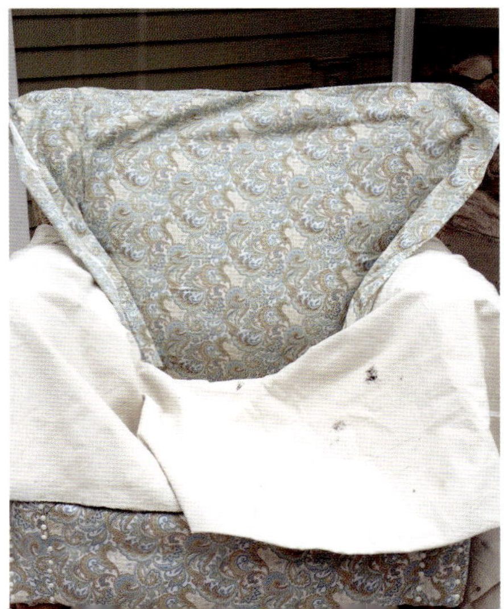

CABINET-TURNED-COFFEE-TABLE

When using salvaged material I always try to think outside the box, but in this case, I worked *with* it! An old wall cabinet found at a recycle center doesn't have to remain a cabinet—turned on its side, it can become a bookcase; on its back it can be a blanket box or coffee table. This modern striped table is just one of the many ways you can repurpose old cabinetry.

Materials

Long cabinet (doors and hinges removed)
Drill
Blue paint (plus small amounts of three other colors)
6 coffee table legs (with flat bases and screw-in brackets)
Electric sander and sandpaper (or hand sand)
Paint brush (and small artist's brush)
Painter's tape
Tarp
Clear glass bumpers
Tempered glass top to cover 3/4 of top

Step 1. Find a cabinet made of solid wood. (Solid wood is better quality than veneer and will be more stable.)

Step 2. Most old cabinets are covered in layers of varnish or paint, so get ready for a fair amount of sanding. You can sand the cabinet by hand or use an electric sander. (If the paint is old, follow lead-paint removal guidelines.) After the varnish or paint has been removed, wipe down the cabinet to get rid of the dust.

Step 3. Next, paint the entire box, along with the feet. Let it dry and then apply a second coat.

Step 4. Use the metal brackets to attach the feet to the bottom of the cabinet (refer to the chicken-coop coffee table project for directions). Longer cabinets may need six feet; for smaller ones you can get away with using only four.

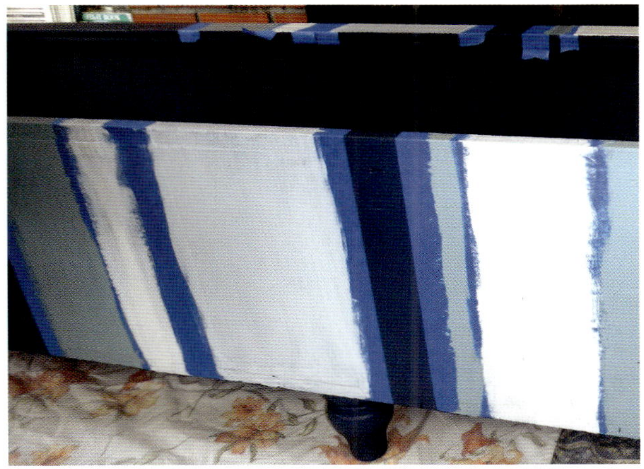

Step 5. Using painter's tape, create a stripe pattern on the cabinet. Mine started and stopped at the salvaged piece of glass I picked up for the top, which covered only part of the cabinet.

Step 6. Paint the stripes in colors that work with the color scheme of your house, letting the paint dry between applications.

Step 7. When the stripes are completely dry, carefully remove the painter's tape. Use a small artist's brush to touch up the lines between colors.

Step 8. Place clear glass bumpers on the top of the cabinet, and lay the glass on top. Add some decor inside the cabinet—I used a houseplant and magazines, but follow your imagination!

NATURE'S COLORFUL WALL DECOR

Do-it-yourself salvage projects aren't always about the big stuff, as this easy, fun project proves. Just like builders, masons, and homeowners buy a little extra tile or hardwood when putting down floors or tiling a bathroom, many crafters buy a little extra yarn or other supplies when making a sweater or quilt. And instead of throwing that extra material away, many donate it to their local thrift store or recycle center. I've purchased bags of yarn, scraps of fabric, and much more in the craft section of recycle shops. For this project I used multiple colors of yarn, but you can easily change the look by changing the colors.

Materials

2 branches
A bag of second-hand yarn
Hot glue gun and glue sticks
Scissors
Picture hanging wire
2 picture-frame hooks

Step 1. Find some sticks with as much character as possible. Make sure they're not too brittle—otherwise they'll break as you work with them.

Step 2. Cut a piece of yarn long enough that you can wrap it around the stick numerous times, and attach the end of the yarn to the stick with the hot glue gun.

Step 3. Begin wrapping the yarn around the stick. If the piece of yarn winds up being too short, just cut another piece and hot glue it on the stick where the first piece ended.

Step 4. Once you have the desired length of color, cut the yarn and hot glue the end down. Start the next color slightly above it, wrapping the new piece downward over the first color and then back up to give a smooth transition. At the branch intersections, wrap back and forth until the branch is covered.

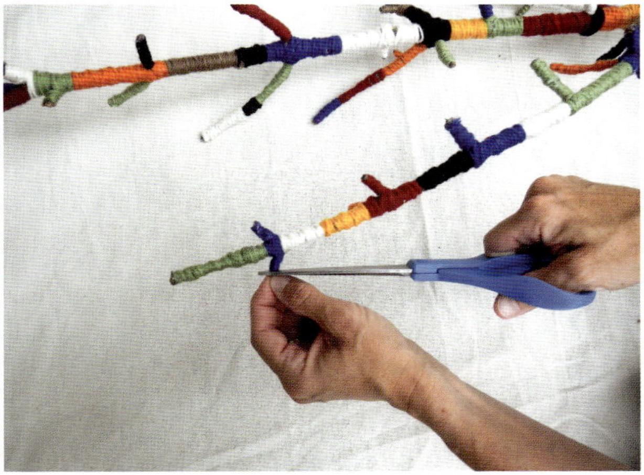

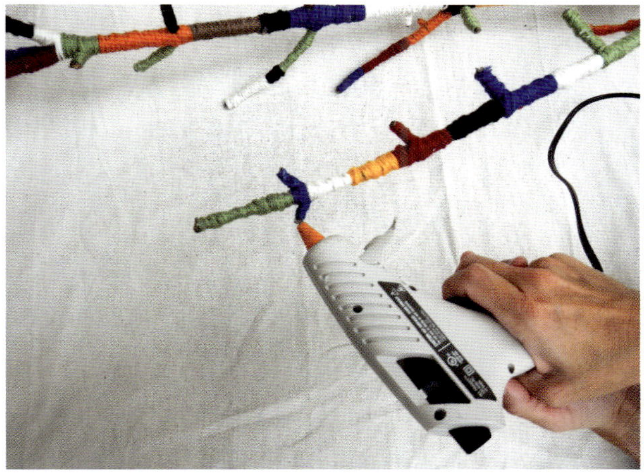

Step 5. Continue wrapping the yarn until only a tiny bit of branch is left at the end. Glue the yarn down, cut it, and then use the scissors to cut off the exposed branch end.

Step 6. Once you cut the branch, place a drop of hot glue on the end to keep the yarn from sliding off. Keep working your way up the branch until it's completely covered. Hang the branches with a little wire and the picture-frame hooks.

SHABBY CHIC CHANDELIER

When I'm not scouring vintage lighting shops and antique centers for gorgeous fixtures, one of my favorite things to do is liven up everyday, basic ones. Paint it pink and adorn it with zebra-stripe ribbons and black pearl drops for a zany look or paint it navy blue and attach little white anchors for a nautical look. Recycled light fixtures can go from blah to wow with a little work and creativity. As you look at the fixtures in your recycle shop, remember to think about what they *can* be rather than what they currently are.

Depending on where you go, often the rebuild center or second-hand shop can test the light fixture for you. Test all the bulbs before you buy the piece to see if it needs to be rewired or is ready to go as is. (If it's a ceiling fixture, the shop owner can attach a plug and plug it in to test the bulbs.)

I bought this light fixture for $15 at the Rebuild Center in Burlington, Vermont. I tested the bulb fixtures to make sure they worked before I left the shop.

Materials

Recycled brass fixture
Steel wool
Rag
Tarp
Metal spray paint primer
Metal spray paint
Recycled electrical wire (with plastic coating)
Wire cutters
Hot glue gun and glue sticks
Old jewelry beads and necklaces
Ribbons and accessories
Candelabra bulbs (25 watt)

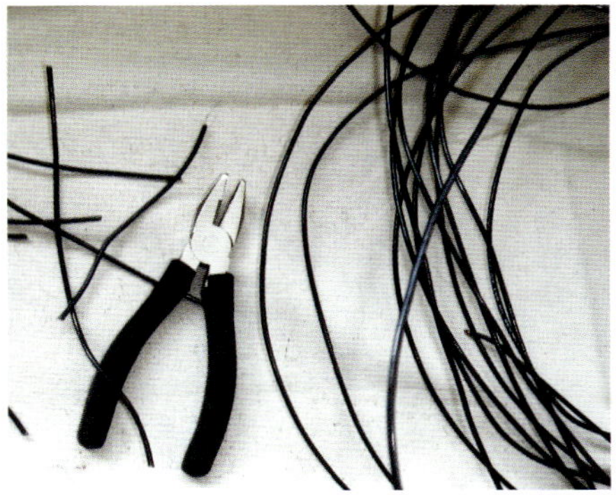

Step 1. I started by removing the glass globes, which I donated back to the rebuild center. I then cleaned the entire fixture, scrubbing it with steel wool and making sure to get into all the nooks and crannies. I then went over it with a damp rag and let it dry completely.

Step 2. Next, I cut recycled electrical wire into 6-inch strips and sanded the strips with steel wool to give them a rough texture that paint would be able to adhere to.

Step 3. I then bent the strips into flower-petal shapes and glued the ends inside the metal cups where the glass globes used to sit.

Step 4. After covering the electrical parts of the fixture (where the light bulbs go) with paper, I hung the fixture outside, sprayed it with metal primer, let it dry, and then sprayed it with a coat of white paint. After the first coat of paint was dry, I sprayed it again, until it was fully covered.

Step 5. Then it was time to add some bling. Along with some 25-watt candle-shaped bulbs, a few old necklaces and pieces of ribbon hung from the arms and tied around the top chain to cover it added that perfect touch of glamour.

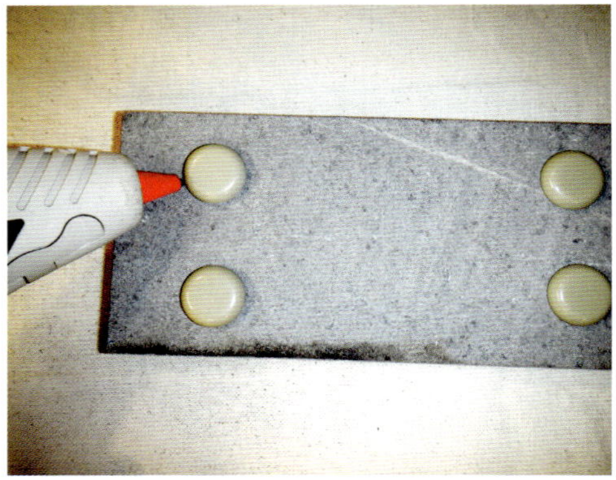

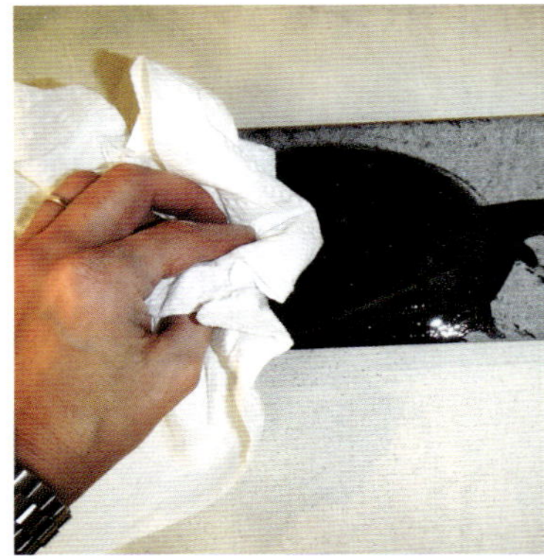

CHEESE PLATTERS AND TRIVETS

Even small, "leftover" pieces of salvage are well worth saving. Many kinds of beautiful stone (marble, granite, slate, soapstone) can be found in architectural salvage shops and rebuild centers. Sometimes there's enough for a backsplash or shower base, but other times only one or two pieces are available. It's time to put them to good use. A perfect gift, these platters or trivets will be a huge hit!

Materials

Scrap of stone
Felt or plastic feet with adhesive backing
Sand paper
Mineral oil
Rags
Hot glue gun and glue sticks

Step 1. Clean the piece of stone with soap and water and let it dry. If you're working with a soft stone like soapstone, you can sand it down and even round the edges off a bit.

Step 2. Attach the feet (most of them are self-adhesive) and reinforce them by going around the edges with a hot glue gun.

Step 3. To seal the platter, pour on a little mineral oil and spread it with a rag. (I use only mineral oil as a sealant because the platter will have food on it.) You don't need a sealant if the stone is going to be used as a trivet (hot plate), but the mineral oil will give it a nice finish so it doesn't hurt to add it. Place some artisan cheeses on it and wrap the whole thing with a piece of cheesecloth and ribbon, and you've got a lovely gift that will delight a hostess with even the most discriminating taste.

COUNTRY MAP TABLE

Salvaged materials are often most beautiful left in their natural state, but when they aren't, a little decoupage can work wonders. I found this table for $7 at Goodwill. Someone had drawn hearts all over it, but it was a sturdy table with fold-down sides. I used country maps for this table, but you could also use wrapping paper, tissue paper, or holiday paper for a table for your Christmas tree. For a wedding, you could even cover the table in white paper, ask all the guests sign it, and then seal it as a memento for the bride and groom.

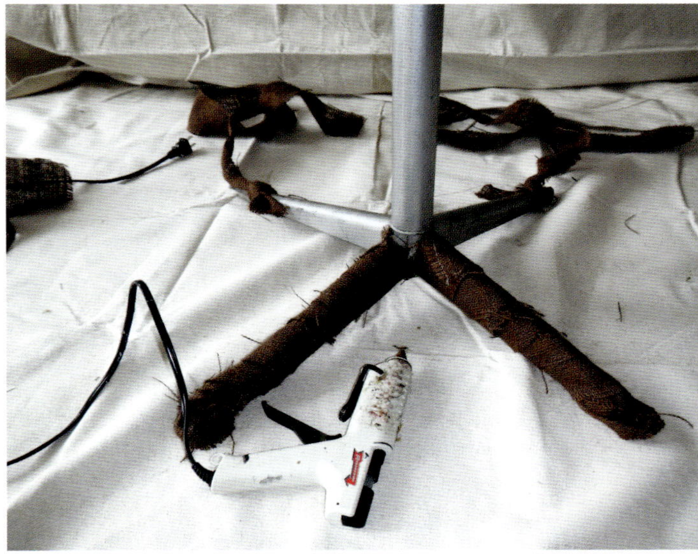

Materials

Second hand table
Maps
Decoupage glue
1 to 2 yards of burlap
Polyacrylic sealant
Stain (optional)
Paintbrush
Scissors
Hot glue gun and glue sticks
Duct tape

Step 1. I first cut up some maps to fit over the top and sides of the table, making sure I left extra for all the edges, include the edge where the table sides folded down.

Step 2. Using decoupage glue and a paintbrush, I brushed the glue on the back of the map as well as on the table and then laid the first map down, smoothing out all the bumps with my hand. Once the map was secure, I brushed decoupage glue over the top of the map, making sure to get the edges down.

Step 3. For the first coat of sealant, I mixed a touch of stain with polyacrylic sealant to give an antique look. After the first coat was dry, I used only the polyacrylic for the second coat.

Step 4. I then cut burlap into strips and wrapped it around the legs and base of the table, using the hot glue gun to secure it in place.

Step 5. On the underside of the table, I used duct tape, cut like a ribbon edge, to keep the map secure along the edges.

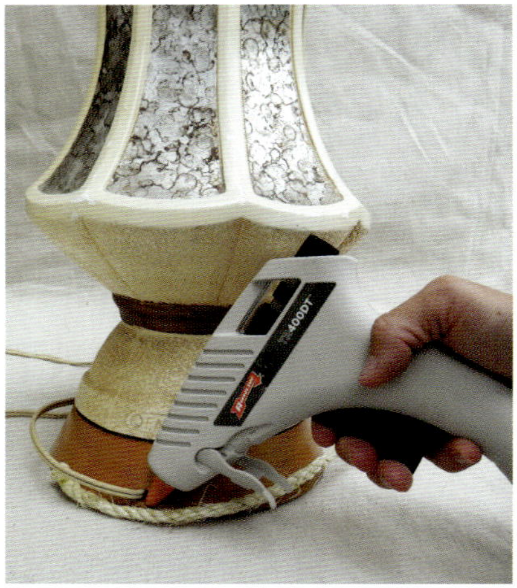

NAUTICAL TABLE LAMPS

Good-quality, second-hand table lamps can be found in abundance at affordable prices. Once you've determined they're not valuable antiques or made by a well-known designer (the lack of a name or stamp on the bottom—or a "Made in China" sticker—is a good indication that they're not valuable pieces), it's time to give them a new look.

Materials

2 lamps
2 lampshades
2 rolls of rope
Hot glue gun and glue sticks
Scissors
1 to 1½ yards of fabric
2 packages of hem/edging trim

This set of sturdy lamps at a recycle shop begged to be taken home. After confirming that they were in working order and that the electrical components weren't loose (which often can be fixed by just tightening the screws), I bought them for ten dollars each.

Step 1. After a good cleaning, starting at the bottom of the lamp, I wrapped the rope around, using the hot glue gun to secure it.

Step 2. As I made my way up the lamp, I continued to push the rope together and hold it in place for a few seconds while the glue dried.

Step 3. I used the shade as a template to cut out a piece of fabric to glue onto it. A little trim around the edge gave it a finished look.

STRIPED AREA RUG

Salvaged area carpets—whether they're antique Orientals or midcentury modern rugs—can be found in many places, but if you'd rather have a unique carpet not previously used by anyone else, you don't have to look any further than a carpet remnant. Many carpet manufacturers and recycle centers have leftover or seconds remnants that are a good size for area rugs. I made a rug similar to the one described here, though much larger, for the DIY NETWORK. Deciding on the pattern you want and the size of the rug is really the hardest part.

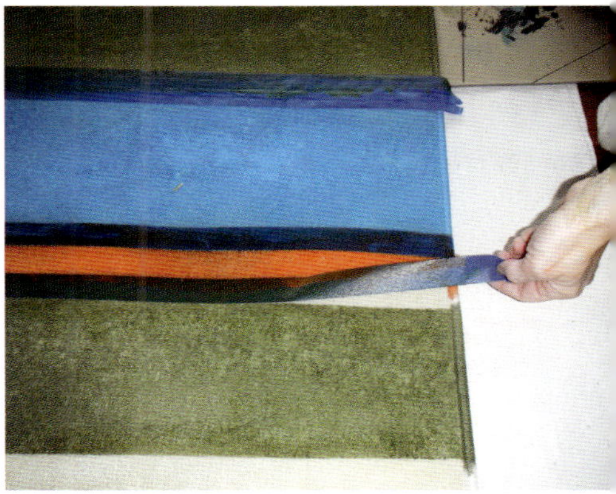

Materials

One solid-color carpet remnant
2 rolls of painter's tape
2 tarps
Many paper bags (or more tarps)
3 to 4 cans of upholstery spray paint (one for each color)

Step 1. Find a carpet remnant that's the size you want and is a light, solid color. (If it's too dark, you won't be able to see the colors you put on it.) Some carpet-remnant stores will bind the edges for you (for a small fee) to give the piece a more finished look. Place the remnant on a couple of tarps.

Step 2. Using painter's tape, mask off the end of the rug so the first color is the original rug color. Then, using a measuring tape and pen, measure out where you want the end of your stripe to be. Random widths of painter's tape and open rug will give you a nice pattern. If you want the pattern to be more symmetrical, do the same measurements on each side and move in toward the middle.

Step 3. Complete the entire pattern with the painter's tape. Make sure the tape is pushed down so the paint doesn't seep under it.

Step 4. Cover both sides of the stripe with paper bags or tarps, placing the bags as close as possible to the edge of the tape to prevent the paint from getting on the other striped areas. Spray one stripe on each side and let them dry before moving on to the next stripe. Wipe excess paint off the tape so that it doesn't drip onto the stripes when you lift the tape up.

Step 5. When the paint is completely dry, carefully remove the tape.

ECLECTIC PRIVACY CURTAIN

Have a boring bathroom shower door or a room that may need a little privacy when guests come to stay? Easy. With an eclectic privacy curtain, you can liven up any room with just a few salvaged textiles.

Textiles are the easiest recycled material to find. Pillowcases, leftover fabric scraps, vintage sheets, old quilts, ripped jeans—these and more can be found at any resale shop or sometimes even in your attic. Mixing and matching a variety of patterns, colors, and shapes gives this curtain its own special look and makes it easier to get all the fabrics you need in one shop. Even with very little sewing skill, you can make this curtain in just a few hours.

Materials

One twin sheet
Assorted fabric scraps (pillowcases, sheets, napkins, t-shirts, old jeans—whatever you want to use)
Sewing machine
Thread
Pins
Scissors
Ironing board and iron
Tension curtain rod
10 clip-on curtain rings

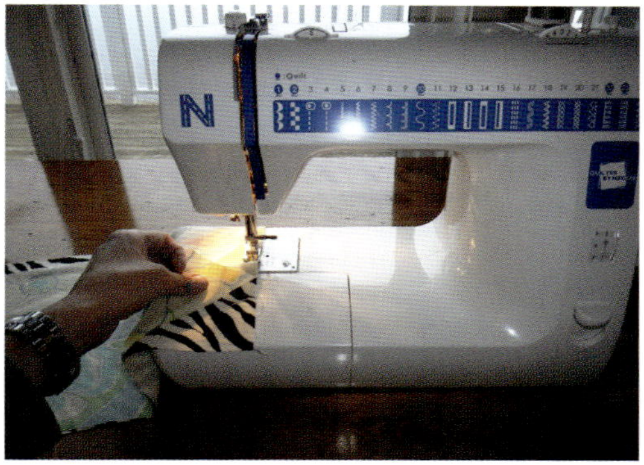

Step 1. I started this curtain by picking up an embroidered pillowcase, an old pair of jeans, some quilt squares, and a checkered twin sheet at my local second-hand shop. I then washed and dried the fabrics—not only to clean them but also to make sure that none of them would shrink when I washed the curtain in the future.

Step 2. I then cut out a number of pieces from the variety of fabrics, keeping the width the same but varying the length. I knew I'd need about 30 pieces so I cut out about 20—this allowed me to lay out the first group and then decide which patterns would best fill in the gaps.

Step 3. After ironing each piece, I placed the pieces face to face on the sides where the widths matched and sewed them to form several strips of fabric. I ironed each seam flat as I went along.

Step 4. Once I finished a row, I laid it out on the sheet to see if I needed another piece and to figure out which strips to place next to the other strips. You don't want two of the same fabrics touching each other. If your sheet is too wide for your project, you can trim the edges with pinking shears or cut and sew an edge.

Step 5. After I completed all the rows, I pinned them down (one at a time) to the twin sheet and stitched each panel down, leaving a little bit of space in between to allow the fun pattern of the sheet to show through.

Step 6. The clip-on curtain rings can be added after the stitching—including along the top and bottom of each row—is complete. Slide the rings over the tension curtain rod and you have a one-of-a-kind privacy curtain.

CLIVE CUSSLER

INSTANT ROMANTIC HEADBOARD

Hollow-core doors used to be the norm—now when people talk about them, they cringe. In fact, so many people are removing their hollow-core doors that many recycle centers won't even take them, leaving homeowners no other option but the dump. But some recycle centers, artists, and builders are becoming very creative with these maligned doors, including The Rebuilding Center in Portland, Oregon, which, with help from local schools, uses them to create attractive wall hangings for sale during fundraisers.

With a little paint or decoupage, hollow-core doors can be used as headboards. Glue on an entire black-and-white photograph or paint on large colorful flowers for a 70s look, or apply some tissue or other decorative paper for a romantic look.

Materials

2 or more hollow-core doors or panels
Screwdriver
8 to 10 sheets of tissue paper
Decoupage glue
6 to 8 1¾-inch screws
Paintbrush
Measuring tape

These hollow-core panels were from a rebuild center. They once were bedroom closet doors.

Step 1. Remove all the hardware from the doors and donate it back to the rebuild center.

Step 2. Pick out some beautiful tissue paper at your local paper shop (or online) and gently tear it into a variety of sizes.

Step 3. Brush the decoupage glue onto the hollow-core panel and on the back of the tissue paper. Place the pieces of paper on the panel in a random fashion, allowing them to overlap slightly. Gently brush more decoupage glue on top of the paper, making sure to cover the edges.

Step 4. Find the center of the bed and place the middle panel on the wall at that spot. Using a 1¾-inch screw, screw the panel onto the wall near the bottom of the panel. Do the same near the top. Then, working out from the center, screw each panel into place, making sure to push the panels together tightly to minimize the seam. Then cover the screws with a little extra tissue paper and glue.

REVAMPED DINING CHAIR

One of the fastest ways to change the look of your dining room is to revamp the chairs. With a little paint and a bold fabric, you can go from outdated to outstanding. Have a cottage-style home? Use a white rough linen. Going for an eclectic look? Paint identical chairs in different colors, or paint mismatched chairs all the same color. Getting creative with outdated dining chairs will not only help reduce waste but also create fun talking pieces.

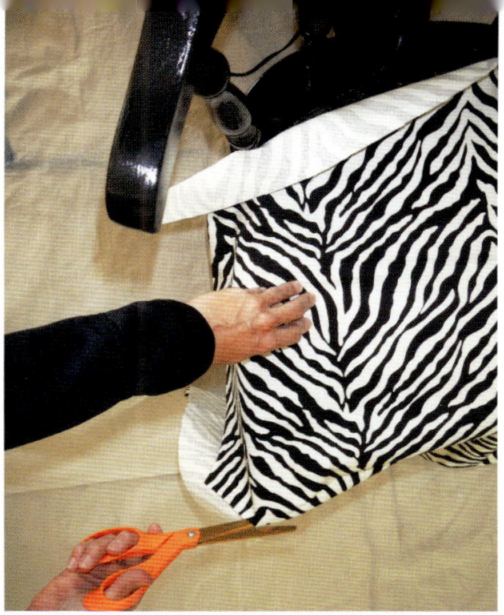

Materials

- Recycled dining chairs with padded seats
- Medium-grain sandpaper
- Black glossy paint
- Paintbrush
- Rags
- Drop cloth
- Fabric for seat cover
- Small pliers
- Staple gun
- Hot glue gun and glue sticks
- Black upholstery nails
- Scissors
- Hammer

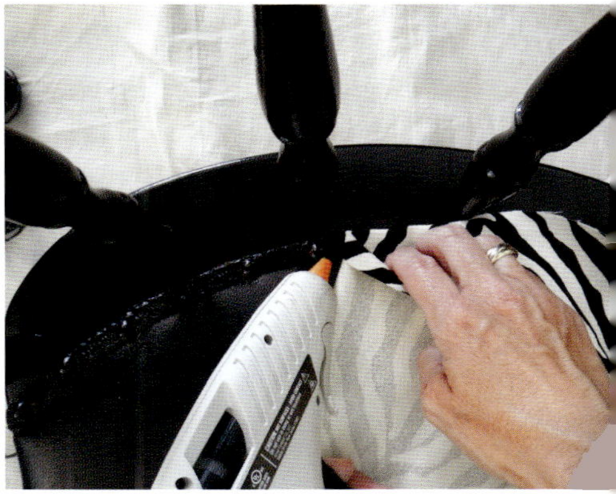

Step 1. Start by sanding the chair with the sandpaper. Once the finish is removed, wipe the chair down well, place it on the drop cloth, and begin applying the black paint. You will need at least two coats.

Step 2. Using the chair seat as a guide, cut the fabric, leaving extra for the back and to wrap under the bottom of the chair.

Step 3. Fold the fabric to give it a clean edge and use the hot glue gun to adhere the fabric around the back of the chair seat, going right over the upholstery nails.

Step 4. Once the back of the seat is covered, smooth out the fabric and carefully wrap it under the chair (using the hot glue to keep the top in place before you turn the chair over). Staple the fabric to the bottom of the chair, cutting any excess off. Then use the hot glue gun to glue down a clean edge.

Step 5. Finally, turn the chair right-side up and insert the black upholstery nails along the back (making sure they go between the ones under the fabric). Use pliers to hold the nail in place while you hammer it.

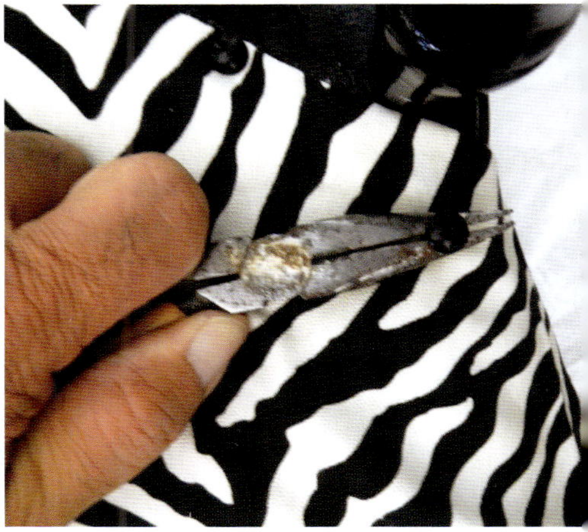

 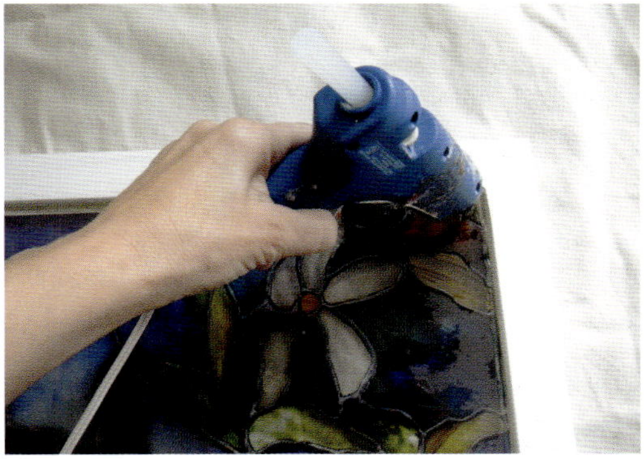 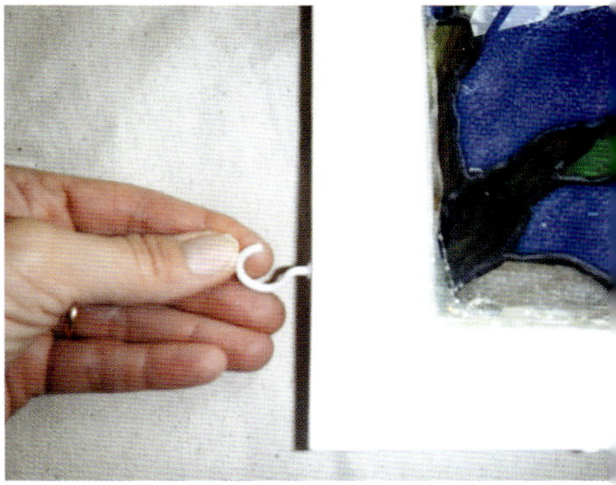

STAINED-GLASS PRIVACY WINDOWS

Old frames and windows are also widely available salvaged goods. Older windows are usually single-pane and not efficient enough to be reused as exterior windows, but they can be used in abundance for interiors. These easy-to-make privacy windows add style to any room.

Materials

Three old frames (with glass) or windows of the same size
Stained-glass decorative window film
White paint
Sandpaper
X-acto knife or scissors
12 coffee-cup hooks (or stronger hooks for larger windows)
3 yards of thin white chain
Measuring tape
Marker
Paintbrush
Wire cutters
Hot glue gun and glue sticks

Step 1. Find three wooden frames (with glass) that are the same size. Clean the frames and remove the inside mats (you can donate them back to recycle shop). Sand the frames so that the paint will adhere, and then paint them white, covering both the front and back. Let them dry and then apply a second coat.

Step 2. Remove the paper backing from the stained-glass film and carefully lay the film over the glass, smoothing out any bubbles. Lift it carefully and start again if it isn't straight.

Step 3. Then, use an X-acto knife to cut the excess film around the edges of the glass. (If you don't have an X-acto knife, scissors will work.)

Step 4. Place the stained-glass film and glass back in the frame. Apply hot glue around the edge to keep the glass in place and give the back a clean look (as it will be seen from outside).

Step 5. Gently twist in the hooks, spacing them evenly across the top of the frame. Cut the chain with wire cutters to fit the height you want. Add hooks to the window frame and hang.

Once an auction coordinator, homeowner Lori Scotnicki now consults on antique appraisals. Her own home is built with re-planed salvaged wood that once was the siding of an old barn. The hand-hewn post-and-beam ceiling wood is from an 18th-century home that was taken down—thankfully a local antiques dealer collected all the lumber before it was thrown away. The furnishing details are vintage pieces that Lori acquired through the years. Her 1930s Chippendale-style dining set once belonged to her grandparents. The bowl on the table is part of Lori's ever-growing yellowware collection. The English dresser was picked up at an auction, along with the old deed stacking boxes. Lori made the fish rug and found the chair at an auction and had it recovered. The table lamp is from the early 1900s and the side table is from the 1840s.

Where to Find Salvage

When it comes to salvaged, reclaimed, and vintage material, it's impossible to list all the resources available—antique shops, vintage shops, recycle shops, repurpose shops, architectural salvage shops, metal shops, and stores and artisans that sell and make products from reclaimed goods are just a few of many. And then there are the online sites, as well as sites dedicated to reclaimed lumber and vintage and recycled furniture. Antique fairs, flea markets, auctions, garage sales, yard sales, and local dumps are other useful places to search. I've found fantastic salvage at the side of the road, usually under a hand-drawn "free" sign. Even your own attic may house long-forgotten hand-me-downs.

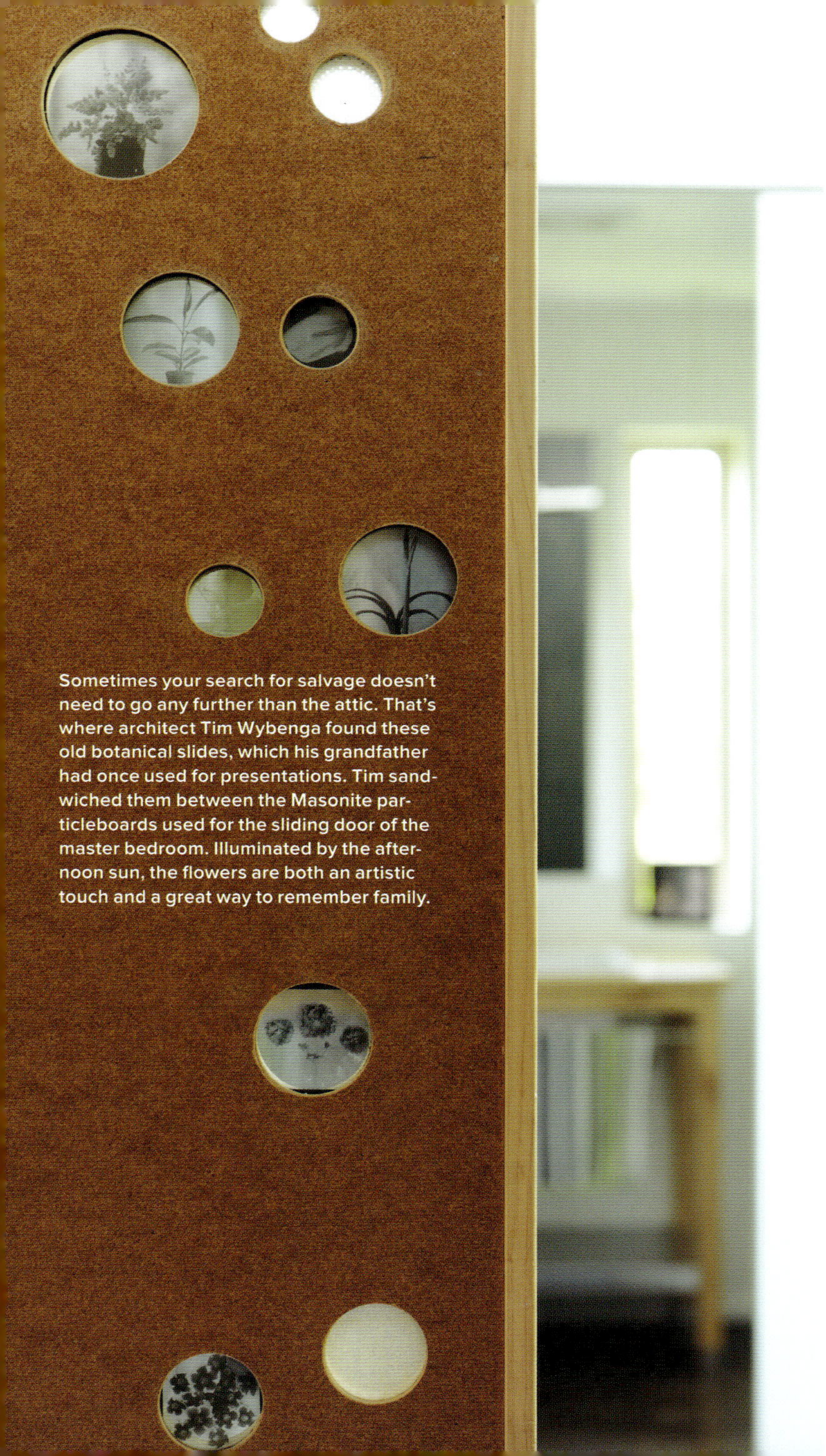

Sometimes your search for salvage doesn't need to go any further than the attic. That's where architect Tim Wybenga found these old botanical slides, which his grandfather had once used for presentations. Tim sandwiched them between the Masonite particleboards used for the sliding door of the master bedroom. Illuminated by the afternoon sun, the flowers are both an artistic touch and a great way to remember family.

Although offering a comprehensive list is impossible, this chapter will give you information about a variety of places to visit in your search for salvage. (The Resources list following this chapter provides names of specific companies, shops, and markets across the country.) With this list to spur you on and generate ideas, you'll be able to spot your own local salvage resources much more easily. I'll also talk about how to envision the numerous uses and design possibilities of salvage. Understanding the "who, where, and how" of salvage will help you become a better detective.

ARCHITECTS, DESIGNERS, AND BUILDERS

Lots of architects, designers, and builders know where to find some of the best salvaged material available. Many of them even buy great pieces when they find them, hoping they'll be able to use them for future client projects. I've seen entire barns filled with amazing salvaged finds waiting to be used. Once you find the experts in your area that work with salvage material, ask them to help you find exactly what you are looking for. Where to get a vintage soapstone sink, how to make fixtures from old gym lights, or even where you can get your grandmother's couch reupholstered—these are all questions that local designers and builders may be able to answer.

This chalkboard above the coffee bar was made by Vermont Farm Table, a company that specializes in making tables and other products out of reclaimed wood. Simple touches like this make this area stand out and add a creative detail.

FONSECA
PORTO
2003
VINTAGE PORT
Gypsy Dancer
Estates
ORENO
TENUTA SETTE PONTI
Baron de L

REBUILD CENTERS

At a rebuild center you can find "everyday" building materials, such as dimensional lumber, double pane windows, trim, tile, cabinetry, sinks, doors, lights. Here it is harder to find the more ornate pieces such as fireplace surrounds and mantels, chandeliers or glass door knobs, as these pieces are usually at architectural salvage shops. But this doesn't mean they won't ever show up. Whether the rebuild center deconstructed a home and they are selling reclaimed material or a builder or homeowner has left over bricks, tile, or even an extra window or two, this is the place to find it. Material turns over fast at these locations, especially vintage pieces, like a barn door with slider or a soapstone sink, so plan to visit often.

Rebuild Centers can be a non-profit or for-profit company. Many of the non-profit centers also have back to work programs, where they train individuals in the building trade. They may be hired to deconstruct a home or remove cabinets during a remodel to bring back to their shop for someone else to reuse. Often the individual who is donating the material will receive a tax deduction. Many of these locations also have a drop off or pick up service for a small fee, making it much easier to use or donate salvage.

Recently, I was walking through an antique fair and overheard the people in front of me talking. A woman pointed out some old windows and exclaimed, "I love those!" to which her friend replied, "Oh, I wish I had known, I just threw fifty of them away." I cringed. Those windows could have easily been brought to the rebuild center, saving her the expense of dumping them, reducing the impact on our environment, earning her a tax write off, and providing her friend with just the sort of salvage find she was looking for. It is a full circle and I hope that more and more people will begin to see it that way.

DESIGN TIP

Most architectural salvage shops and rebuild centers know the designers and builders who work with salvage material because they frequent their shops. Ask the people at the shop for recommendations. Don't forget to look at the architect or designer's portfolio. Does it highlight salvage? If not, is the designer or architect willing to work with it?

◀◀ This kitchen was a labor of love, with each piece of salvage puzzled together by homeowner Mary Atwood. Mary chipped the old grout off of salvaged slate tiles she picked up at the rebuild center before laying them down for the floor. Built by George Ramos Woodworking, the custom cabinetry was made from reclaimed fir and incorporates old wine boxes from Mary's uncle's winery. Mary found the vintage gas stove on Craigslist. The counters are remnant pieces of SlateScape. The cabinet above the counter was picked up at a garage sale for $10 and painted black. The green metal base of the table was once part of an old French bistro table, and the accessories were found at a bunch of garage sales.

ARCHITECTURAL SALVAGE SHOPS

Architectural salvage stores are some of the best places to visit to find goods for your home design. Structural materials such as beams, doors, and flooring, as well as sinks, cabinetry, and hardware are in abundance, and they are usually more unique and historically significant than those at a rebuild center or recycle shop. When buildings need to be demolished due to the environmental conditions of an area, a change of use, or because the building has been deemed unsafe, the experts at architectural salvage shops carefully remove the structural elements, marking where they came from and often repairing or restoring them before they are even put on the floor for sale. The deconstruction, transportation, labor, repair, and retail space are all costly, but that extra expense means that these significant architectural pieces can be used once again. If you'd like these types of architectural pieces in your home, make sure to budget for them—and allow them to be key elements in the design. They are worth it.

▲ Rejuvenation in Portland, Oregon (see p. 135), is one of hundreds of architectural salvage shops across the nation. Some of the most unique and valuable architectural and historic salvage pieces can be found at these shops.

◀ Nearly 100% percent of the furnishings in Jane Coslick's shabby chic cottage living room were salvaged or created by local artists (see p. 191). She reupholstered the old couch in funky fabrics, found a bunch of vintage signs and paintings, an old desk and second-hand office chair, and replaced all the doors in the cottage with vintage hardwood ones.

NONPROFIT SECOND-HAND STORES

One of my favorite second-hand stores is located in the side of a church building. It has an inconspicuous metal door with no sign other than a small plaque reading "shop open" on the two days a week when it operates. These little boutique second-hand shops run by volunteers are all unique. Once you start to frequent them, you'll get a better sense of what you can find at each. Some I go to just for clothing and textiles; others I frequent for furniture. But almost inevitably, I find a surprise—something I would have never expected to stumble upon at that particular location. That's the thing about second-hand stores—you never know what is going to be brought in. Goodwill, Salvation Army, Habitat for Humanity, local charity shops, and churches are just a few of the places you can find second-hand treasures. Make a list of the ones in your area, as well as when they're open. Many are open only a few times a month or even a year, and some have a big sale ($1 per bag) on certain dates. Get the scoop and don't miss out!

VINTAGE, ANTIQUE, AND SECOND-HAND SHOPS

Vintage, antique, or recycled-goods shops are similar to their nonprofit counterparts but are privately owned. At nonprofits, you donate your items and get a tax write-off, whereas privately owned stores will give you cash or a consignment value for the items you bring in. These stores are usually more predictable and in their hours and what they carry, unlike the nonprofits, which can be very hit or miss in what they have. Also, whereas employees as at nonprofits usually won't keep a lookout for a particular piece you want because too many people come and go, a for-profit store with one owner may consider looking for a piece for you on commission or even setting something aside when it comes in. But nonprofit or for-profit—both are important parts of the reuse industry and provide jobs and small business opportunities.

Many of these shops specialize in certain periods or styles of furniture and other goods, whether it's midcentury modern or early American antiques. High-end designer boutiques are fairly common in bigger cities, as well as funky used-clothing stores that are likely to have fabrics for a "mod" pillow project or something similar. I've used large retro skirts (which can have up to 3 yards of fabric) to make pillows, napkins, and even a curtain for under a bathroom sink.

DESIGN TIP

Goodwill's mission is to provide vocational opportunities to people with barriers to employment, and other nonprofits like Salvation Army and Habitat for Humanity are equally invested in helping to provide jobs and training to people in the community. And across the nation, these stores collect hundreds of millions of pounds of second-hand items that would otherwise end up in our landfills. Finding a great bargain, being eco-conscious, and supporting a great cause: It's a win-win-win! Most second-hand shops have items that are donated from within a few miles of their location, so if you know the neighborhood, you know what quality and items you are likely to find in the shop.

RETAIL SHOPS

That's right—more and more retail shops are now carrying one-of-a-kind salvaged or recycled items in their stores (and online). From well-known brands to smaller independent shops scattered across the country, these retail stores are capitalizing on salvage, not only in the design of their spaces, but also in their merchandise.

But take note—some stores make items that look old when they actually aren't. If you're specifically looking for something that is vintage or made from recycled material, ask a salesperson about the product you are looking at. Otherwise it's hard to tell the difference between something that's truly an eco-friendly recycled piece and something that just appears to be.

▲ The Lounge Lizard, located in Portland, Oregon, specializes in midcentury modern and retro goods. The shop is full of great lighting, tables, and furniture. This pair of matching upholstered side chairs—hard items to find together—would look great recovered in a fun retro pattern. They are good quality, comfortable, and a great size.

◀ Sheridan + Company, in Seattle, is just one of the many independent boutique retail shops that sell vintage, antique, and salvaged furnishings and decor alongside new products. Even larger retailers like Rejuvenation, West Elm, Pottery Barn, Anthropologie, Restoration Hardware, ABC Carpet & Home, and the like are selling vintage and recycled pieces next to their new items. Retailers and customers are seeing the appeal in vintage and one-of-a-kind pieces.

SPECIALIZED SECOND-HAND WAREHOUSES AND SUPPLIERS

There's more? Yes, there is! Specialized second-hand warehouses and suppliers carry goods salvaged from specific kinds of businesses and institutions. Some colleges and universities, for example, have warehouse sales of the items they are no longer using for the school. Lab chairs, old blackboards, desks, tables, metal lockers, lamps—you name it. If it's a school-related item you're after, it could be offered at one of these sales. Used-office-furniture stores also have a wealth of great finds—I've turned old office credenzas into home bars or open shelving for kitchens and pantries. A second-hand restaurant supplier is a great place to get stainless steel tables, big pots and pans, and sets of chairs that you can reupholster. Think about the material or product you want and ask around for specialized places that might sell it secondhand.

SPECIALTY MATERIAL COMPANIES

Are you looking for a specific material—a copper pipe for a do-it-yourself pot-rack project, for example, or a shipping container to be insulated and wired for electricity by your builder? Who in the world sells used copper pipes or steel containers? These aren't things you can pick up at your local second-hand shop. It might take a bit of work to find the right supplier, but these types of specialty material companies and stores are becoming increasingly popular. Start by asking local designers, or try an Internet search.

A Google search may pull up a list of places that sell steel containers six states away, but many times you can find whatever you're looking for locally. The storage-unit facility on the other side of town may not have a website or even an email address, but a dozen steel containers might just be sitting in its back lot. Don't be afraid to do a little detective work. If I were looking for a copper pipe, for example, I'd start by contacting a local metalworker to ask if he sells salvaged copper pipe. Even if the answer is no, that person might know someone who does. If I were looking for a shipping container, I'd contact a local truck company. They might have one or point me in the right direction. It may take a few phone calls, but you won't know if you don't try.

Once you've found a place that carries the material you're looking for, it's

DESIGN TIP

Most people think of second-hand or antique stores for what we in the industry call "smalls" (little stuff like plates, knickknacks, and so on). But some of the best furniture can come from these places as well. Some second-hand shops are dedicated solely to larger home decor items. Not sure where they are in your area? An online search for "used furniture store" is a good place to start.

▲ Recycled glass tile can be found in any shape, size, and color at Bedrock Industries, an artisan recycled-glass-tile company. Whether you're looking for sea-glass subway tile for a kitchen backsplash or designing a bathroom with an all-white shower surround, recycled glass tiles can help you get as funky, retro, modern, or contemporary as you desire.

▶ Bamboo Revolution carries a product called "a scrap top," a post-consumer recycled countertop made from discarded end cuts of woven flooring. These countertops can be up to 15 feet long and 7 feet wide. Here is a sample board of a "scrap top" counter are beautifully displayed on the company's own countertop made with concrete and slices of bamboo. You can choose a varnish, oil, or other type of finish depending on the look you want (and on wear-and-tear considerations).

important to remember that they may have restrictions about walking around (due to liability issues) or they may be open only certain times of the year. Checking out the scrap metal shop in your area? Call ahead and, by all means, dress appropriately (close-toed shoes, long sleeves, and work gloves). Many of these places don't deal directly with the public, so don't assume that they take credit cards—plan ahead!

RECYCLED-PRODUCT COMPANIES

Subway tiles made from recycled street lights, countertops made of recycled bamboo end-cuts, rain gutters made from wine bottles, sinks from old aluminum screens, light fixtures from recycled metal, floor tile from old toilets—companies are transforming old materials into new products in hundreds of inventive ways. When you don't want a salvaged look or even a unique salvaged piece, you can still use recycled products that are eco-friendly but look contemporary.

ARTISANS

Artisans can make some amazing pieces out of recycled material. Sometimes they have a store (online or brick-and-mortar), but you can also find them through local contacts or shows. Keep a list of specialized stores in your area—lighting, glass, woodworking, metalworking, upholstery, vintage, and antiques.

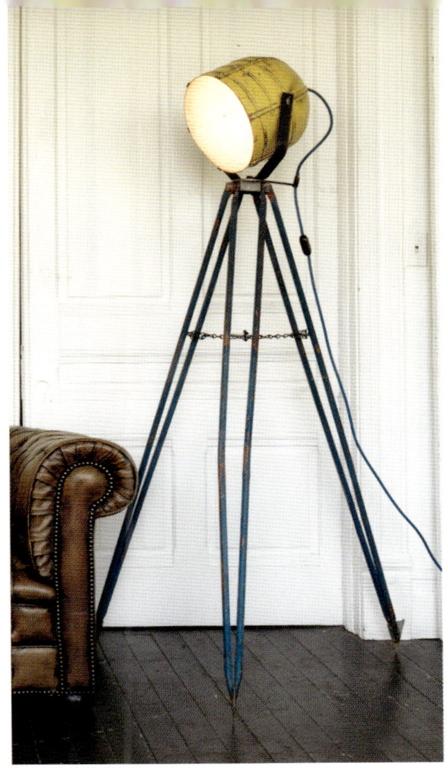

Andy Whitcomb of Whitcomb & Company in Seattle is a furniture designer who creates unique pieces out of local reclaimed material. He is a shining example of stellar design with sustainable materials. Andy sells his creations at local stores and online, proving that you can make a living in the recycle field. This floor lamp (above) was made with an old surveyor's tripod and part of a scuba air tank.

Besides supporting your local community, by incorporating artisan-made products you are supplying the demand necessary to bring fresh new ideas to the salvage world.

Stephanie Larrowe, owner of TOTeM Salvaged, works out of her Los Angeles home, using vintage and salvaged materials like blankets and embroidery to create one-of-a-kind accessories as well as to re-cover second-hand furnishings. Filled with vintage fabrics, blankets, belts, and buckles, this small room in her home workshop is where the magic happens. Her living room, featured in Chapter 3, showcases her creativity when it comes to mixing vintage furniture and bright vintage textiles.

ONLINE SOURCES

Craigslist, eBay, Etsy, Fab, One Kings Lane, South of Market, Goodwill, 1stdibs, Three Potato Four, salvageone, Ruby Lane, and many more—these web-based venues (and dozens more) are ideal places to find second-hand and salvaged goods. Plus, dozens of brick-and-mortar retail shops that have a salvage section (like Rejuvenation and Anthropologie, just to mention a couple) also offer their products through their websites. And then there are the many architectural salvage shops, reclaimed-wood companies, vintage lighting stores, and antique stores across the country that have both retail stores and websites. Looking only for midcentury, art deco, or arts and crafts items? Many of these online stores specialize in goods from specific periods.

Anna Palmer collects vintage pieces not only for her own home but also for her online store, Refresh Collections. Many people are moving away from opening brick-and-mortar stores and are instead selling their salvaged and vintage collections directly to consumers online. These online "stores" are beautifully curated and can help you find very specific items. Many sites, like Anna's, specialize in barware, textiles, furniture, paintings, and books from a particular time period. If you're looking for something older and unique, don't forget to check these smaller online sites.

FAIRS, SHOWS, AND MARKETS

Most people who enjoy vintage, antique, or salvaged pieces have heard of Brimfield (in Massachusetts), the Country Living Fairs (in New York, Ohio, and Georgia), Round Top (in Texas), or 127 Flea (the world's largest flea market at 690 miles long, stretching from Michigan to Alabama). Fairs, markets, and shows are wonderful places to shop for unique pieces (see the Resources section that follows this chapter). The advantage to large shows is that you can find everything from complete dining sets to salt-and-pepper shakers, but even small shows will offer a range of goods. Building materials (such as salvaged boards and tile pieces) are rare at these shows (though not unheard of), but you'll find table after table filled with great vintage and salvaged decor. When you head out, make sure you have a list of the dimensions of pieces you're looking for, and a tape measure, cash (in case the booth doesn't take credit cards), and a car or truck that's large enough to transport your purchases. (And don't forget to wear comfortable shoes!) There are two schools of thought for these shows— arrive early to get the good stuff, or arrive late to get the deals. My own feeling is just go with what works for you! (See the "Guided Walkthrough" later in this chapter for more tips on how to approach antique fairs and flea markets.)

Because I was giving a presentation at this Country Living Fair in Atlanta, I was all dressed up. But usually when I shop at flea markets or antique shows, I wear jeans, rubber boots, a rain jacket, and a hat. These picture frames would be perfect for the DIY project I tackled in Chapter 7 (see p. 236).

These circa 1900s Denton New York State Fish and Game Department prints, collected over a number of years, were found at various locations, including auctions, antique shows, shops, and online sites. Once the homeowner had collected twelve, she framed them with a burlap mat to add texture. The collection now hangs in the master bedroom.

AUCTIONS

Auctions can be a terrifically fun experience. But be open-minded, because it's impossible to know what you'll come away with, and be patient, because waiting for the piece you want to bid on can take a long time. Many people bring reading, work, or something else to do (like knitting) while they wait. Some auctions offer online bidding for those who can't come to the auction house—you can set up an account to bid online and follow the auction live on your computer from the comfort of your own home. Telephone bidding is also an option—you can arrange ahead of time to have an employee at the auction house bid for you while you're on the phone with that person. But it's best to make a live appearance at the auction house, if you can, so you can touch and see the items in person. Photographs of items can be deceptive, especially if they're not high quality images—an antique lamp or rug may look great in a catalogue or online but just ho-hum in person. If you can't make it to the auction itself, it's worth attending the preview beforehand, when the house opens its doors for people to see the items before they hit the bidding floor.

A GUIDED SHOPPING TRIP

One of the most popular events I've led was a guided walkthrough with a group of people at a rebuild center. They loved it and the recycle center still talks about how informative and inspiring it was. I pointed out items that the attendees wouldn't have looked at twice otherwise, talked about how the look of certain salvaged pieces could be changed, and offered thoughts on how to use items in imaginative ways.

Even when they're creative and committed, people who are new to salvage hunting may simply not know where to begin. If this sounds like you, come along with me on the following salvage-store walkthroughs.

Rebuild Center Walkthrough

You can come across entire stone countertops at rebuild centers or architectural salvage shops, like this one, Build It Green! NYC, in Brooklyn. Most are the same width but some are extra deep, so you should double-check the size. If the size is too big, you can cut it down. Some stones, like soapstone, are easy to cut—you can push the pieces together and hide the seams with colored epoxy. If it's a hard stone, contact your local mason or stoneyard to get an estimate for having the stone cut to the exact dimensions you need or just into counter width (usually 24x24-inch) tiles.

New tempered glass for shower walls, shelving, or tabletops can be expensive—picking up a recycled piece is sometimes only a tenth of the cost. This recycled glass is ready to be installed. If you need it cut, many glass places will cut it for you for a fee. Tempered glass is much harder to cut than plate glass so it should be cut by a professional. Use it for a shower wall or a coffee table top.

Build It Green!NYC, in Brooklyn, has a seemingly endless collection of tubs and sinks of every style—modern acrylic soaker tubs, a Jacuzzi, a vintage cast-iron tub that needs a little sandblasting and repair, freestanding cast-iron sinks, drop-in bowls and stainless-steel double sinks, vintage sinks with built-in backsplashes and aprons, and more. All you need to know is what your design measurements are, what style you're looking for, and whether you want something that's ready to go or are able to spend a little time and money on a more unusual piece that's in need of repair.

Most of the time rebuild centers have regular household goods and materials for everyday living, but keep your eyes peeled for unusual pieces. These extra-large brackets would be amazing for a storefront sign—or set on a fireplace mantel for an industrial decor look if you have high ceilings. You could have them sandblasted and repainted or just clean them up and let the patina of their age shine through.

Wall sconces, lamps, and ceiling fixtures are in abundance at rebuild centers. Most will be more recent seconds from the 1970s, 80s, and 90s, which you can repurpose like I did in Chapter 7 (see p. 244), but sometimes you'll come across a rarer piece. Many of these light fixtures are just waiting to be upcycled into something more modern and hip.

▸ I picked up all ten of these clear-glass vases, in varying shapes and sizes, at my local second-hand shop. Each is nothing special on its own, but grouped together and holding the same type of flower, they make for a beautiful display. The clear-glass tabletop they're set on lends a nice visual consistency and allows the natural light to refract through the display.

▾ Goodwill hunting! Like many second-hand stores, this Goodwill had shelves and shelves of vases. Seeing so many pieces at once can be overwhelming, so it's important to be organized in the way you look through them. Remember, it's more about finding the right *combination* of vases than it is about spotting any singular great piece. Figure out a strategy—maybe you look only for vases in solid, bright colors. Maybe it's all clear-glass vases, or only pink ones in various materials. Pull the vases off the shelves and begin putting them together in sets of three, five, seven, or eleven (yes, odd numbers are better). This will give you a good sense of which look best together.

Second-Hand Store Walkthrough

Second-hand shops should come with a warning—"Addictive!" Something new (or should I say old) often appears in them everyday. It is hard not to want to swing by to make sure you're not missing anything. Some second-hand shops are very organized, with kitchen items in one place, textiles in another, and pictures and frames in yet another area, but others are just rambling piles of stuff. Once you familiarize yourself with your local second-hand shop you'll realize that the search is half the fun. But also realize that these shops do much more than provide home furnishings for the curious shopper—they help reduce waste and provide jobs and training, and loads of goods at a deep discount. It is a win-win-win.

When I look at blankets, curtains, or even clothing I do it with an eye toward what else they can be used for. Bedding doesn't have to go on the bed, and curtains don't have to go on windows—a blanket might be perfect as upholstery material for a second-hand chair (see p. 172) or as an instant headboard framed in a box of salvaged wood. Think of the pieces as fabric, particularly if they have holes or tears that would need to be cut off. I especially appreciate needlepoint and crewelwork—handmade pieces you don't often see anymore because of the amount of time and precision they require. You may not want to display them in a frame on the wall like your grandmother did, but that doesn't mean you can't use them in some other way, like for an accent pillow on the bed. You can give the frame back to the second-hand shop or use it in a different way.

The people who have booths at antique fairs and flea markets may also have a shop (brick and mortar or online), or they may regularly attend other fairs and markets in the area, so if you find a booth with stuff you like, make sure you get their card so you can find them again. Even if they don't have exactly what you're looking for on that day, they'll continue to stock salvaged goods that are your style. These doors and shutters, rare reclaimed material finds at the Summerhouse booth at the Country Living Fair, would make great signs, tabletops, or closet doors.

I always look for frames at second-hand shops. Don't worry about whether you like the art inside—frames with depth and texture can be used as decor themselves. Paint them all the same color and line a wall with them or layer them inside one another (see p. 236). New frames are usually very expensive, so getting them at second-hand shops is smart.

◂ Textiles, especially old quilts in need of repair, can be great finds—like this one for only $15 at the Rosa Bergen Antiques booth. The prices are usually good and you can find so many uses for them. Even with its tears, this quilt could be framed on a wall in a cottage, or made into extra-large pillow shams. A lot of work goes into vintage quilts, many of which are hand-stitched.

Antique Fair or Flea Market Walkthrough

If someone had given me the tips I am about to pass along to you, my first few experiences at antique fairs and flea markets would have been much more pleasant. Here are a few of the basics you should know before you head out.

Wear the right footwear. The grounds are usually all dirt (not grass), and a recent rain can make them pretty muddy. Wear waterproof shoes that have traction, a lot of support, and are comfortable. You could be walking around for hours, and you don't want your feet to stop before you are ready to.

Park nearby. Spend a few extra dollars on the closest parking lot. This way you can drop stuff off at your car or truck at regular intervals, and if you need a little catnap or break for a snack, you don't have far to go. Arrive early to get parking close to the area where you are going to shop.

Scout booth locations ahead of time. Most shows have a list of vendors, and with a little online research you can figure out which ones you want to visit and where they are located in the fair layout. If you're going to check the fair out, with no agenda for particular items, then just hit a few sections (many fairs are too big to see everything) and write down the names of your favorite booths so you can find them the next year (they won't always be in the same place).

Go with someone who can be independent. Fairs have a variety of goods, and

◂◂ Former NASCAR racer Shawna Robinson loves big, bold, crazy colors. As the creator of Happy Chairs, she sells re-covered vintage chairs at shows like the Country Living Fair, as well as online and at retail locations. At the show, you get a sense of her style as well as an opportunity to chat with her and her "crew" about other pieces that are available or even about custom work. For many vendors, the show is just one way to get their upcycled and repurposed products to the public.

the booths that interest you may not interest the friend or family member you came with. Staying attached at the hip will be unpleasant for both of you. So pull out your cell phone (or walkie-talkie if there's no cell reception) and wander through the booths independently. You can call each other if you wander too far apart.

Bring cash. Cash is king at fairs and markets. Many vendors are able to process credit cards with apps on their smartphones, but don't count on that every time, especially when you're buying small-ticket items or are at a show in a more rural area. If you forget to bring cash with you, ask whether the show has an ATM—most larger ones do.

Interesting architectural and vintage or antique pieces can always be found at the Rhine River Antiques booth. This large wall chart, one of many in the Rhine River collection, was once used in a school in Europe. It would be perfect in a coastal home on the wall in a dining room or above an extra-large fireplace. Offbeat pieces like this one make designing with salvage so much fun. Decor doesn't have to end at landscape paintings and flower vases—be different and make your home your own by finding salvaged items that are like no other.

Haggling is allowed, but be courteous. Don't be competitive, aggressive, or downright rude when you try to negotiate. Remember, the vendors are just trying to make a living and between the cost of the booth, the cost of transporting the goods, and the time they're spending to be there, turning even a meager profit isn't always easy. Imagine if a client walked into your place of business and said something like "This dental cleaning isn't worth more than $25" or "I'm not paying more than $50 for that legal consultation"! A better approach is to politely ask, "Would you be willing to take $25 for this?" If they say no, then answer with, "I really appreciate your considering it," and walk away if you don't want to pay their price. (By the way, this polite and positive approach goes for every shop at which you try to negotiate, whether a recycle center, salvage shop, antique shop, or other.)

Bring plenty of water, sun block, and a hat. You won't believe how thirsty you get. If it's a hot day, fill bottles with ice and leave a bunch in your car. When you go back to drop things off, grab a fresh one for your backpack. Wear a ball cap rather than a wide-rimmed hat so that your hat doesn't get in everyone's way in a small tent or booth.

Bring a pushcart with wheels or a large backpack. Trying to carry everything in your arms becomes next to impossible after a few purchases. If you can carry it in a backpack or pushcart, your hands will be free to check out all the goods. Many fairs are now offering drop off places where you can leave your purchases so you don't have to lug them around. You can make drop offs as many times as you want until you are ready to leave.

Bring a big car or truck, or befriend someone who has one. You'll need it to take your purchases home. If you are flying to the show, find out their shipping policies in advance.

Have a great time! Fairs and markets are crazy, busy places and you have to embrace the chaos. Don't get upset by traffic, people crossing the road, busy booths, or the like. Smile and have fun. You'll meet some amazing people.

An entire room could be designed around this fantastic chandelier I spotted in the back of the Dove Cote booth. Take the time to check out the larger goods at fairs.

Renee Tornabene, a design student and blogger, has been mixing and matching salvaged material since she was a kid. With her recent move to Phoenix she turned a plain-Jane condo into a cozy home that looks like it belongs on the cover of a shabby chic magazine. A vintage bottle holder and mirror, a collection of old photographs, salvaged cupboards from all periods (some painted and some distressed), and a two-toned antique dining table come together to create a dining area that is warm and inviting.

Resources

Repurposing, salvaging, and recycling is not just a fad—it's the way we have to live our lives if we are to tread more gently on this earth. My hope is that this book will inspire you to do just that. Whether you're reusing something as simple as a glass jar in your decor or incorporating salvaged brick, wood, and metal in the architecture of your home or business, you can appreciate the beauty of reclaimed materials.

Modern-day building practices that don't incorporate salvage are taking a toll on our resources and energy consumption. But taking just a few small steps toward thinking about what goes in our homes will make a huge difference in the entire design and build industry. As this book shows, many talented artisans, builders, designers, architects, and companies specialize in the reuse of what we already have available today. Take advantage of their knowledge, skill, and design talent and change the way you build and decorate your home. Let them be your guide.

Many of the individuals and companies listed here are the same ones who created the designs pictured in this book (see the Credits). But this list is by no means exhaustive; there are hundreds more around the country, and I'm sorry I couldn't list them all.

The resources are grouped into two categories:

Architects, Designers, Stylists, Design-Build Companies, and Builders. Remember, even though we list office locations, many people travel for their work—regionally, nationally, and even internationally. Don't hesitate to be in touch with them even if they're not located near you.

Places to Purchase Salvaged Goods and Goods Made of Salvaged Materials. This section includes architectural salvage shops, rebuild shops, and restore centers; antique and vintage shops; flea markets and antique fairs; secondhand shops; online shops; companies and stores that sell new products made of salvaged material; and companies and stores that sell new products, salvaged goods, and goods made from salvaged material. The brick-and-mortar locations of these places are listed, but many sell (and will ship) across the nation through their websites. Much of the decor featured in this book comes from these companies or was mentioned to us by one of the salvage designers listed. If you're interested in a certain piece or look from the book, check out the Credits to see who (or what company) designed it, and look here for their contact information.

ARCHITECTS, DESIGNERS, STYLISTS, DESIGN-BUILD COMPANIES, AND BUILDERS

Annette Joseph
Atlanta, Georgia
www.ajphotostylist.net
Stylist

Arciform
Portland, Oregon
www.arciform.com
Design-build

Austin Restorations
Phoenixville, Pennsylvania
www.austinrestorations.com
Cabinet refinishing

Bamboo Revolution
Portland, Oregon
www.bamboorevolution.com
Design and product

Birdseye Building Company
Richmond, Vermont
www.birdseyebuilding.com
Design-build

Cady Construction
Seattle, Washington
cadyconstruction@gmail.com
Builder

Conner and Buck Builders
Bristol, Vermont
www.connerandbuck.com
Design-build

The Cushman Design Group
Stowe, Vermont
www.cushmandeisgn.com
Architecture and design

Czopek & Erdenberger
Portland, Oregon
www.czopek.com
Design

Daniel Hale Furniture Design/ Interior Design/Architecture
San Francisco, California
www.danielhale.com
Design

Daniel Smith & Associates Architects
Berkeley, California
www.dsaarch.com
Architecture

David Rush General Contractor
Portland, Oregon
www.rushtobuild.com
Design-build

DRW Design/Build
Portland, Oregon
www.drwdesignbuild.com
Design-build

Elizabeth Herrmann Architecture + Design
Bristol, Vermont
www.eharchitect.com
Architecture

Erin Martin Design
St. Helena, California
www.erinmartindesign.com
Design

Ernest R. Munch Architect Urban Planner
Portland, Oergon
www.ermunch.com
Architecture

George Ramos Woodworking
Portland, Oregon
www.georgeramoswoodworking.com
Cabinetry

Green Hammer Construction
Portland, Oregon
www.greenhammerconstruction.com
Builder

Gristmill Builders
Stowe, Vermont
www.gristmillbuilders.com
Builder

Heidi Arnold Design
St. John, Virgin Islands
www.heidiarnolddesign.com
Architecture

Hunter Lane Interiors
Laura Hollister-Takashima
Portland, Oregon
503-901-5757
Interior design

Integrity Construction
Winooski, Vermont
802-373-7334
Builder

Jane Coslick Designs and Restorations
Savannah, Georgia
www.janecoslick.com
Design and restoration

Jane Kim Design
New York, New York
www.janekimdesign.com
Design

J.A.S. Design Build
Seattle, Washington
www.jasdesignbuild.com
Design-build

Jessica Helgerson Interior Design
Portland, Oregon
www.jhinteriordesign.com
Design

Jim Huntington, Design/Build
Charlotte, Vermont
www.jimhuntingtondesignbuild.com
Design-build

Joan Heaton Architects
Bristol, Vermont
www.joanheatonarchitects.com
Architecture

Joanne Palmisano
Burlington, Vermont
www.joannepalmisano.com
Designer and stylist

Karin Lidbeck-Brent
Cape Cod, Massachusetts
www.lidbeckbrent.com
Stylist

Kelly and Abramson Architecture
Piedmont, California
www.kellybramson.com
Architecture

Kelly G Design
New York, New York
www.kellyg-design.com
Design

Kelly LaPlante
Austin, Texas
www.kellylaplante.com
Design

Langford Construction
LaGrange, Georgia
www.dnlangford.com
Builder

Laura Migliori & Peter Brevig Architects
Portland, Oregon
503-228-4921
Architecture

Lewis Creek Builders
North Ferrisburg, Vermont
www.lewiscreekbuilders.com
Builder

Lori Scotnicki
Champlain Valley Area, Vermont
www.vermontada.com
Antique appraiser

McLeod Kredell Architects
Middlebury, Vermont
www.mcleodkredell.com
Architecture

Melissa McCall Design
Portland, Oregon
www.mccalldesignllc.com
Design

Michael Minadeo + Partners
Essex Junction, Vermont
www.minadeopartners.com
Architecture

Michelle de la Vega Interior Design
Seattle, Washington
www.michelledelavega.com
Design

Mitra Designs Studio
Bristol, Vermont
www.mitradesigns.com
Architecture

Nathan Good Architects
Portland and Salem, Oregon
www.nathangoodarchitects.com
Architecture

Neil Kelly Design/Build/Remodeling
Portland, Oregon
www.neilkelly.com
Design-build

North Woods Joinery
Cambridge, Vermont
www.nwjoinery.com
Design-build

Northern Timbers Construction
Ripton, Vermont
www.northerntimbers.com
Builder

Office of Mobile Design
Venice, California
www.designmobile.com
Design

OZ Architects
Scottsdale, Arizona
www.ozarchitects.com
Architecture

Peregrine Design/Build
South Burlington, Vermont
www.peregrinedesignbuild.com
Design-build

Pill-Maharam Architects
Shelburne, Vermont
www.pillmaharam.com
Architecture

Pomerantz Woodworking
Fayston, Vermont
www.perantzwoodworking.com
Builder

Poutre's Design
Scottsdale, Arizona
www.poutresdesign.com
Cabinetry

Ramsay Gourd Architects
Manchester and Burlington, Vermont
www.rgavt.com
Architecture

Reclaimed Space
Austin, Texas
www.reclaimedspace.com
Builder

Rich Elstrom Construction
Gearhart, Oregon
www.richelestromconstruction.com
Builder

Robinson Hill Architects
Costa Mesa, California
www.rhainc.net
Architecture

Sandy Koepke Interior Design
Los Angeles, California
www.sandykoepkeinteriordesign.com
Design

Select Design
Burlington, Vermont
www.selectdesign.com
Brand and product development

Selin + Selin Architecture
Shelburne, Vermont
www.selinandselin.com
Architecture

Shannon Quimby
Portland, Oregon
www.shannonquimby.com
Designer and stylist

Shelbyville Remodeling
Portland, Oregon
www.shelbyvilleremodeling.com
Builder

Sheridan + Company
Seattle, Washington
www.sheridaninteriordesign.com
Design

Shover Construction
Shelburne, Vermont
www.shoverconstruction.com
Builder

Silver Maple Construction
Bristol, Vermont
www.silvermapleconstruction.com
Builder

Silver Ridge Design, Inc. Architects
Hyde Park, Vermont
www.silverridgedesign.com
Architecture

Simpson Cabinetry
South Burlington, Vermont
www.simpsoncabinetry.com
Cabinetry

Specialty Design
Jeffersonville, Vermont
www.specialtydesignvt.com
Builder

Square Feet Studio
Atlanta, Georgia
www.squarefeetstudio.com
Architecture, planning, and design

Studio III Architects
Bristol, Vermont
www.studio3architecture.net
Architecture

Studio Frederico
Portland, Oregon
wnlwl@yahoo.com
Design

Sweeney Design Build
Shelburne, Vermont
www.sweeneydesignbuild.com
Design-build

Teresa Ridlon Interiors
Tempe, Arizona
www.ridloninteriors.com
Design

TruexCullins Architecture and Interior Design
Burlington, Vermont
www.truexcullins.com
Architecture and interior design

TVA Architects
Portland, Oregon
www.tvaarchitects.com
Architecture

Vermont Case and Cabinet
Starksboro, Vermont
802-453-7669
Cabinetry

Yianni Doulis Architecture Studio
Portland, Oregon
www.ydarchitecture.com
Architecture

PLACES TO PURCHASE SALVAGED GOODS AND GOODS MADE OF SALVAGED MATERIALS

ABC Carpet & Home
New York, New York
www.abchome.com

Adam & Eve
West Palm Beach, Florida
www.adamandevesalvage.com

Adkins Architectural Antiques
Houston, Texas
www.adkinsantiques.com

ADMAC Salvage
Littleton, New Hampshire
www.admacsalvage.com

American Salvage
Miami, Florida
www.americansalvage.com

Amighini Architectural Inc.
Jersey City, New Jersey
www.amighini.net

Amighini Architectural Salvage & Antiques
Anaheim, California
www.salvageantiques.com

Anthropologie
(vintage furnishings)
nationwide stores
www.anthropologie.com

Antiques on Farmington
Farmington, Connecticut
www.antiquesonfarmington.com

Antiquities & Oddities Architectural Salvage
Kansas City, Missouri
www.aoarchitecturalsalvage.com

Architectural Accents
Atlanta, Georgia
www.architecturalaccents.com

Architectural Antique Warehouse
Fairhope, Alabama
www.siteone.com/shop/architectural

Architectural Antiques
Minneapolis, Minnesota
www.archantiques.com

Architectural Antiques Exchange
Philadelphia, Pennsylvania
www.architecuralantiques.com

Architectural Antiques of Indianapolis
Indianapolis, Indiana
www.antiquearchitectural.com

Architectural Antiquities
Harborside, Maine
www.archantiquities.com

Architectural Artifacts
Chicago, Illinois
www.architecturalartifacts.com

Architectural Artifacts
Denver, Colorado
www.architectural-artifacts.com

Architectural Elements
Sioux Falls, South Dakota
605-339-9646

Architectural Emporium
Canonsburg, Pennsylvania
www.architectural-emporium.com

Architectural Old House Parts
Front Royal, Virginia
www.oldhouseparts.net

Architectural Salvage Inc.
Exeter, New Hampshire
www.oldhousesalvage.com

Architectural Salvage, Inc.
Denver, Colorado
www.salvagelady.com

Architectural Salvage of Greensboro
Greensboro, North Carolina
www.blandwood.org

Architectural Salvage of San Diego
San Diego, California
www.architecturalsalvagesd.com

Architectural Salvage Warehouse
Essex Junction, Vermont
www.greatsalvage.com

Architectural Salvage Warehouse of Detroit
Detroit, Michigan
www.aswdetroit.org

Architectural Salvage, W.D.
Louisville, Kentucky
www.architecturalsalvage.com

Artefact Design & Salvage
Sonoma, California
www.artefactdesignsalvage.com

Aurora Mills Architectural Salvage
Aurora, Oregon
www.auroramills.com

B&C Emporium
Allegan, Michigan
www.b-c-e.biz

Barge Canal Market
(vintage furnishings)
Burlington, Vermont
www.bargecanalmarket.com

Barntiques
(furniture made of reclaimed wood)
New York, New York
www.barntiques.com

Barnwood Industries
(reclaimed wood)
Bend, Oregon
www.barnwoodindustries.com

Bedrock Industries
(recycled-glass tiles)
Seattle, Washington
www.bedrockindustries.com

Big Daddy's Antiques
San Francisco and Los Angeles, California
www.bdantiques.com

Black Dog Salvage
Roanoke, Virginia
www.blackdogsalvage.com

The Brass Knob
Washington DC
www.thebrassknob.com

Brown Elephant Resale Shops
Chicago, Illinois
www.howardbrown.org

Build It Green!NYC
Queens & Brooklyn, New York
www.bignyc.org

Builders Trading Company
Encinitas, California
www.builderstrading.com

Building Materials Resource Center
Boston, Massachusetts
www.bostonbmrc.org

Capitola Freight & Salvage
Santa Cruz, California
www.capitolafreight.com

Caravati's Inc.
Richmond, Virginia
www.caravatis.com

Carolina Architectural Salvage at Cogan's Antiques
Ridgeway, South Carolina
www.cogansantiques.com

Champlain Valley Antique Center
Shelburne, Vermont
www.vermontantiquecenter.com

Church Mouse
Palm Beach, Florida
www.bbts.org

City Salvage
Minneapolis, Minnesota
www.citysalvage.com

Cline's Country Antiques
North Carolina
www.clinesantiquesmpnc.com

Community Forklift
Edmonstron, Maryland
www.communityforklift.com

Conant Metal & Light
(vintage lighting and lighting made from repurposed salvage)
Burlington, Vermont
www.conantmetalandlight.com

Construction Junction
Pittsburgh, Pennsylvania
www.constructionjunction.org

Cornerstone Inc.
Cameron, North Carolina, and Brooklyn, New York
www.cornerstonesalvage.com

Cowgirl Attic
Lexington, Kentucky
www.cowgirlattic.com

Cross Creek Architectural Artifacts
Springfield, Missouri
www.crosscreekartifacts.com

Crossland Studio
Charlotte, North Carolina
www.yp.bellsouth.com/sites/crossland

Demolition Depot
New York, New York
www.demolitiondepot.com

Discount Home Warehouse
Dallas, Texas
www.dhwsalvage.com

Discovery Architectural Antiques
Gonzales, Texas
www.discoverys.com

District Millworks
(reclaimed wood)
Los Angeles, California
www.districtmillworks.com

Doc's Architectural Salvage
Indianapolis, Indiana
www.docsarchitecturalsalvage.com

Earthwise Architectural Salvage
Seattle, Washington
www.earthwise-salvage.com

Eleek Inc.
(sinks, lights, and hardware made of recycled aluminum)
Portland, Oregon
www.eleek.com

Endurawood
(reclaimed wood)
Portland, Oregon
www.endurawood.com

Fifi's Salvage
Augusta, Maine
www.fifisalvage.com

Finger Lakes ReUse
Ithaca, New York
www.fingerlatereuse.org

Fireclay Tile
(tiles made of recycled glass and ceramic)
San Jose and San Francisco, California
www.fireclaytile.com

Five Corners Antiques
Essex Junction, Vermont
www.fivecornersantiques.com

FLOR
(recycled carpet squares)
nationwide stores
www.flor.com

Freeway Building Materials
Los Angeles, California
www.freewaybuildingmaterials.us

George's Architectural Salvage
Salt Lake City, Utah
www.georgessalvage.com

GleenGlass
(recycled-glass products)
Vancouver, Washington
www.gleenglass.com

Goodwill
nationwide stores
www.goodwill.org

Green Demolitions
Connecticut and New Jersey
www.greendemolitions.org

The Green Project
New Orleans, Louisiana
www.thegreenproject.org

Greenwich Hospital Thrift Shop
Greenwich, Connecticut
www.greenhosp.org

HeritageCo2
Royal Oak, Michigan
www.heritageco2.com

The Heritage Company
Kalamazoo, Michigan
www.heritagearchitecturalantiques.com

Hippo Hardware & Trading Company
Portland, Oregon
www.hippohardware.com

Historic Albany Foundation Architectural Parts Warehouse
Albany, New York
www.historic-albany.org

Historic Houseparts
Rochester, New York
www.historichouseparts.com

Historic Houston Salvage Warehouse
Houston, Texas
www.historichouston.org

Historic York Architectural Warehouse
York, Pennsylvania
www.historicyork.org

Housewerks
Baltimore, Maryland
www.housewerksalvage.com

Housing Works Shops
stores throughout New York City
www.housingworks.org

IceStone
(recycled-glass and concrete counters)
Brooklyn, New York
www.icestoneusa.com

Inretrospect
Long Beach, California
www.inretrospect.co

Irreplaceable Artifacts
Middletown, Connecticut
www.irreplaceableartifacts.com

Island Girl Salvage
Elk Grove Village, Illinois
www.islandgirlsalvage.com

Lang Farm Antique Center
Essex, Vermont
www.langfarmantiquecenter.com

The Loading Dock
Baltimore, Maryland
www.loadingdock.org

Lot 49
(vintage furnishings)
Oakland, California
www.lot-49.com

Lounge Lizard
(vintage furnishings and lighting)
Portland, Oregon
www.facebook.com/loungelizardvintage

Mason Brothers Architectural Salvage Warehouse
Essex Junction, Vermont
www.greatsalvage.com

Material Unlimited
Ypsilanti, Michigan
www.materialsunlimited.com

McGee Salvage
(reclaimed wood)
Portland, Oregon
www.mcgeesalvage.com

Metropolitan Artifacts
Atlanta, Georgia
www.metropolitanartifacts.com

Nauticals of Marblehead
(furnishings and bars made of wood from old boats)
Marblehead, Massachusetts
www.nauticalsofmarblehead.com

New England Demolition & Salvage
New Bedford, Massachusetts
www.nesalvage.com

New York Salvage
Oneonta, New York
www.architiques.net

Nor'East Architectural Antiques
South Hampton, New Hampshire
www.noreast1.com

North Shore Architectural Antiques
Two Harbors, Minnesota
www.north-shore-architectural-antiques.com

Off The Wall Architectural Antiques
Carmel, California
offthewallantiquescarmel.com

Ohmega Salvage
Berkeley, California
www.ohmegasalvage.com

Old Globe Wood
(reclaimed wood)
Superior, Wisconsin
www.oldglobewood.com

The Old Home Supply House
Fort Worth, Texas
www.oldhomesupplyhouse.com

The Old House Parts Co.
Kennebunk, Maine
www.oldhouseparts.com

Old House Salvage
Piedmont, South Carolina
www.theoldhousesalvage.com

Old House Society Warehouse
Bloomington, Illinois
www.oldhousesociety.org

Old Portland Hardware & Architectural
Portland, Oregon
www.oldportlandhardware.com

Old Town Architectural Salvage
Wichita, Kansas
www.oldtownarchitecturalsalvage.com

Olde Good Things
Los Angeles, California, New York, New York, and Scranton, Pennsylvania
www.oldegoodthings.com

PaperStone
(recycled-paper counters)
wholesaler
www.paperstone.com

Pasadena Architecural Salvage
Pasadena, California
www.pasadenaarchitecturalsalvage.com

Pieces of the Past
Johnson City, Texas
www.pieces-of-the-past.com

Pinch of the Past
Greensboro and Savannah, Georgia
www.pinchofthepast.com

Pink Pig
(home goods, clothing, and accessories)
Westport, New York
www.pinkpigwestport.com

Portland Architectural Salvage
Portland, Maine
www.portlandsalvage.com

Preservation Hall
Weaverville, North Carolina
www.preservation-hall.com

Preservation Station
Nashville, Tennessee
www.thepreservationstation.com

Provenance Architecturals LLC
Philadelphia, Pennsylvania
www.phillyprovenance.com

ReBuild Warehouse
Springfield, Virginia
www.rebuildwarehouse.org

Rebuilding Center of Our United Villages
Portland, Oregon
www.rebuildingcenter.org

Reclaimed Wood Materials
Southern California (and online)
www.reclaimedwoodmaterials.com

The ReCONNstruction Center
New Britain, Connecticut
www.reconnstructioncenter.org

Recycling the Past
Barnegat, New Jersey
www.recyclingthepast.com

The ReHouse Store
Rochester, New York
www.rehouseny.com

Rejuvenation
Portland, Seattle, Los Angeles, Berkeley
www.rejuvenation.com

ReNew Building Materials & Salvage
Brattleboro, Vermont
www.renewsalvage.com

RePurpose
Westland, Michigan
www.repurposeshop.com

Rescued Relics
Montgomery, Alabama
334-240-4512

ReSource
Buffalo, New York
www.buffaloreuse.org

ReSource and ReBuild Centers
Burlington, Vermont
www.resourcevt.org

Restoration Resources
Boston, Massachusetts
www.restorationresources.com

Restoration Warehouse
Dubuque, Iowa
www.restorationwarehouse.net

ReStore
Philadelphia, Pennsylvania
www.re-store-online.com

The RE-Store
Seattle and Bellingham, Washington
www.re-store.org

The ReUse People
Pacoima and Oakland, California
www.thereusepeople.org

ReUse the Past
Grantville, Georgia
www.reusethepast.com

Revival Studio
(furnishings made out of license plates)
Burlington, Vermont
www.revivalstudio.com

Revivals Resale Mart
Palm Springs, California
760-318-6430

Rough Linen
(vintage and new linens)
San Raphael, California
www.roughlinen.com

Rust & Roses
Phoenix, Arizona
www.rustandroses.blogspot.com

Salvage Heaven
Milwaukee, Wisconsin
www.salvageheaven.com

Salvage One
Chicago, Illinois
www.salvageone.com

Salvage with Style
St. Joseph, Michigan
www.misalvagewithstyle.com

Salvage Wrights, Ltd.
Orange, Virginia
www.salvagewrights.com

Salvation Army
nationwide stores
www.salvationarmyusa.org

Sarasota Architectural Salvage
Sarasota, Florida
www.sarasotasalvage.com

Seattle Building Salvage
Seattle, Washington
www.seattlebuildingsalvage.com

Second Chance Inc
Baltimore, Maryland
www.secondchanceinc.org

Second Use
Seattle, Washington
www.seconduse.com

Shabby Chic
(vintage furnishings)
Nationwide Shops
www.rachelashwellshabbychiccouture.com

Shaver Brothers
Auburn, New York
www.shaverbrothers.com

Significant Elements
Ithaca, New York
www.significantelements.org

Silverlake Architectural Salvage
Pasadena, California
www.silverlakesalvage.net

Silver Fox Salvage
Abany, New York
www.silverfoxsalvage.com

Southern Accents Architectural Antiques
Cullman, Alabama
www.antiques-archchitectural.com

Southern California Architectural Salvage
Los Angeles, California
www.socalarchitecturalsalvage.com

Stardust Building Supplies
Mesa and Phoenix, Arizona
www.stardustbuilding.org

The Stock Pile
Canton, Ohio
www.thestockpile.org

Summer Land Style Upholstery
Bellingham, Washington
www.summerlandstyle.com

Taipan Architectural Salvage
Santa Barbara, California
www.taipanarchsalage.blogspot.com

Tillotson Trading Architectural Salvage
East Cornith, Vermont
http://www.tillotsontrading.com

Toledo Architectural Artifacts Inc.
Toledo, Ohio
www.coolstuffiscoolstuff.com

TOTeM
(furnishings reuphostered in salvaged textiles)
Los Angeles, California
www.totemsalvaged.com

Trailer Park
Brooklyn, New York
www.trailerparkslope.com

Treasure City Room Service
Austin, Texas
www.treausurecitythrift.org

Über Chic Home
Salt Lake City, Los Angeles
www.uberchichome.com

Urban Archaeology
New York, New York
www.urbanarchaeology.com

Urban Remains
Chicago, Illinois
www.urbanremainschicago.com

Vermont Farm Table
(reclaimed-wood furniture)
Burlington, Vermont
www.vermontfarmtable.com

Vermont Salvage
White River Junction, Vermont
www.vermontsalvage.com

Vermont WildWoods
www.vermontwildwoods.com

Vetrazzo
(recycled-glass and concrete surfaces)
Tate, Georgia
www.vetrazzo.com

Vintage Brick Salvage
Rockford, Illinois
www.bricksalvage.com

Vintage Inspired Lifestyle Marketplace
Burlington, Vermont
www.vintageinspired.net

Vintage Renewel
(reupholstered furnishings)
Idledale, Colorado
www.vintagerenewal.com

Viridian Reclaimed Wood
www.viridianwood.com

The Weld House
(furnishings made of metal from old cars)
Tempe, Arizona
www.weldhouse.com

West Elm
(reclaimed-wood furnishings)
nationwide stores
www.westelm.com

Whitcomb & Company
(repurposed furnishings)
Seattle, Washington, and Los Angeles, California
www.whitcombandcompany.com

White River Architectural Salvage & Antiques
Centerville and Zionsville, Indiana
www.whiteriversalvage.com

Whole House Building Supply and Salvage
San Mateo, California
www.driftwoodsalvage.com

Woman's Exchange Thrift Shop
Sarasota, Florida
www.sarasotawex.com

Wooden Nickel Antiques
Cincinnati, Ohio
www.woodennickelantiques.net

Zaborski Emporium
Kingston, New York
www.stanthejunkman.com

Directories and Online Shops

1st Dibs
www.1stdibs.com

Buildings Materials Reuse Association (nationwide listing)
www.BMRA.org

Chairish
www.chairish.com

Craigslist
www.craigslist.org

Directory of Architectural Salvage Stores (nationwide listing)
www.oldhousejournal.com

Directory of Reuse People (nationwide listing)
www.thereusepeople.org

eBay
www.ebay.com

Etsy
www.etsy.com

Free Cycle Network
www.freecycle.org

Front Porch Forum
www.frontporchforum.com

Goodwill
www.shopgoodwill.com

Habitat for Humanity ReStores (nationwide listing)
www.habitat.org/restores

One King's Lane
www.onekingslane.com

Reclaimed Architecture
www.reclaimedarchitecture.com

Refresh Collection
(vintage dishware)
www.refreshcollections.com

Rehab Vintage
www.rehabvintage.com

Relique
www.relique.com

Second Shout Out
www.secondshoutout.com

SalvoWeb
www.salvo.com

Three Potato Four
www.threepotatofourshop.com

Two Jakes
www.twojakes.com

Vintage Renewal
www.vintagerenewal.com

Flea Markets and Antique Fairs

127 Corridor Sale
Runs from Michigan to Alabama
www.127sale.com

Alameda Point Antiques Faire
Alameda, California
www.alamedapointantiquesfaire.com

The All Night Flea Market
Wheaton, Illinois
www.zurkopromotions.com

Austin County Flea Market
Austin, Texas
www.austincounty.citymax.com

Brimfield Antique & Flea Market Shows
Brimfield, Massachusetts
www.brimfieldshow.com

Brooklyn Flea
Brooklyn, New York
www.brooklynflea.com

Canton First Monday Trade Days
Canton, Texas
www.firstmondaycanton.com

Chicago Antique Market
Chicago, Illinois
www.randolphstreetmarket.com

Country Living Antique Fairs
Rhinebeck, New York, Columbus, Ohio, and Atlanta, Georgia
www.countryliving.com

Elephant's Trunk Country Flea Market
Milford, Connecticut
www.etflea.com

Hell's Kitchen Flea Market
New York, New York
www.hellskitchenfleamarket.com

The Junk Bonanza
Shakopee, Minnesota
www.junkbonanza.com

Long Beach Antique Market
Long Beach, California
www.longbeachantiquemarket.com

Portland Expo Antique/Collectibles
Portland, Oregon
www.expocenter.org

Raleigh Flea Market
Raleigh, North Carolina
www.raleighfleamarket.net

Rose Bowl Flea Market
Los Angeles, California
www.rgcshows.com

Round Top Antiques Fair
Round Top, Texas
www.roundtop.org

San Jose Flea Market
San Jose, California
www.sjfm.com

Scott Antique Markets
Atlanta, Georgia
www.scottantiquemarket.com

Seattle Antiques Market
Seattle, Washington
www.seattleantiquesmarket.com

Shipshewana Flea Market
Shipshewana, Indiana
www.tradingplaceamerica.com

Springfield Antique & Flea Market
Springfield, Ohio
www.springfieldantiqueshow.com

Upper West Side Flea Market
New York, New York
www.greenfleamarkets.com

Credits

cover	Jessica Helgerson Interior Designs; Yianni Doulis Architecture Studio
p. 1	design, Michelle de la Vega
p. 2	design, homeowner Tricia Rose, Rough Linen
p. 5	lamp design, Andy Whitcomb, Whitcomb & Company
p. 6	design, homeowners Susan Lyon and Tim Wybenga, TVA Architects
p. 8	design, homeowners Susan and Ryan Hayes; builder, Bill Litchfield, Specialty Design Vermont
p. 12	design, Joanne Palmisano
p. 13	industrial letters from Rejuvenation; design, homeowners Rosanne Palmisano and Sean Roy
p. 14	boat bar by Davita Nowland, Nauticals of Marblehead

p. 16 design, Joanne Palmisano, DIY Network Salvage Video Series
p. 19 design, Joanne Palmisano; table, Joanne Palmisano & Shannon Quimby
p. 20 design, homeowner Nancy (blog, Replaceinpdx.com) and Arciform Design/Build
p. 21 design, homeowner Dana; cabinetry, Robert Poutre, Poutre's Design
p. 23 design, homeowners Raymond and Dana Murphy
p. 24 design, homeowners Susan Lyons and Tim Wybenga, TVA Architects
p. 26 design, Jane Coslick Designs and Restoration

Chapter 1

p. 28 design, Jane Kim Design; interior designer, Ben Shulman
p. 31 design, Anna Palmer, Refresh Collections
p. 33 Conner and Buck Builders, Vermont Eco-Floors
p. 34 design, Joanne Palmisano, DIY Network Salvage Video Series
p. 35 design, omeowner Christine Lobel; cabinetry, Vermont Case and Cabinet; architect, Stefan Richter; builder, Shover Construction
p. 36 design, Joanne Palmisano; illustration, Cliff Deetjen
p. 37 photo by Joanne Palmisano
p. 38 design, homeowner Christine Lobel; cabinetry, Vermont Case and Cabinet; architect, Stefan Richter; builder, Shover Construction
p. 39 interior design, Teresa Ridlon, Ridlon Interiors
p. 40 design, Rachael and George Ramos and architect Martin Backenmeyer; cabinetry, George Ramos Woodworking
p. 41 design, homeowner Mary Atwood; cabinetry, George Ramos Woodworking
p. 44 interior design, Teresa Ridlon, Ridlon Interiors
p. 46 interior design, Michelle de la Vega; builder, Cady Construction
p. 48 design, homeowners Raymond and Dana Murphy; cabinetry, Simpson Cabinetry; lighting, Conant Metal and Light
p. 49 (top) interior design, homeowner Christine Lobel; cabinetry, Vermont Case and Cabinet
p. 49 (bottom) design, Jane Kim Design; interior designer, Ben Shulman; table, Barntiques.com
p. 50 interior design, Colleen Frederick, Studio Frederico; builder, Mark Asiano
p. 51 (top) design, homeowners Raymond and Dana Murphy
p. 51 (bottom) design, homeowner Christine Lobel; cabinetry, Vermont Case and Cabinet; architect, Stefan Richter; builder, Shover Construction
p. 53 interior design, Michelle de la Vega; builder, Cady Construction
p. 54 interior design, Joanne Palmisano; builder, New England Housewrights; architect, Silver Ridge Design
p. 56 design and cabinetry, homeowner Robert Poutre, Poutre's Design
p. 57 design, Anna Palmer, Refresh Collections
p. 59 design, Jane Coslick Designs and Restoration

Chapter 2

p. 60 design, Jane Coslick Designs and Restoration
p. 63 birch wall cabinet, homeowner Lori Scotnicki and William Mahoney Renovations
p. 64 design, Joanne Palmisano; illustration, Cliff Deetjen
p. 65 (left) design, Renee Tornabene, BulbtoBlossom.com
p. 65 (right) design, Susan Lyons and Tim Wybenga, TVA Architects
p. 66 design, Joanne Palmisano; illustration, Cliff Deetjen
p. 67 design, homeowner Nancy, designer Anne DeWolf, and Arciform Design/Build
p. 68 design, Jane Coslick Designs and Restoration
p. 69 interior design, Annette Joseph
p. 70 interior design, Teresa Ridlon, Ridlon Interiors
p. 72 interior design, Anna Palmer, Refresh Collections
p. 73 interior design, homeowner Lori Scotnicki; builder, Dave Warick, DW Construction
p. 74 interior design, Michelle de la Vega; builder, Cady Construction
p. 75 interior design, Annette Joseph
p. 76 interior design, Joanne Palmisano; builder, New England Housewrights; architect, Silver Ridge Design
p. 77 interior design, homeowner Lori Scotnicki; builder, Dave Warick, DW Construction
p. 78 Arciform Design/Build
p. 79 Arciform Design/Build
p. 80 design, Michelle de la Vega; builder, Cady Construction
p. 81 design, Teresa Ridlon, Ridlon Interiors
p. 82 Arciform Design/Build
p. 83 design, homeowner Christine Lobel; architect, Stefan Richter; builder, Shover Construction
p. 84 (left) design, Annette Joseph
p. 84 (right) design, Colleen Frederick, Studio Frederico; tiling, Hugh Frederick, Deco Stone & Tile
p. 85 design, Joanne Palmisano; illustration, Cliff Deetjen
p. 86 design, Jane Coslick Designs and Restoration
p. 87 design, homeowner Nancy, Anne DeWolf, and Arciform Design/Build
p. 88 (left) design, homeowners Dana and Raymond Murphy
p. 88 (right) design, homeowner Kerri Hoyt-Pack, Anne DeWolf, and Arciform Design/Build
p. 89 design, Jane Kim Design; interior designer, Ben Shulman
p. 90 design, homeowner Kerri Hoyt-Pack, Anne DeWolf, and Arciform Design/Build
p. 91 design, homeowner Kerri Hoyt-Pack, Anne DeWolf, and Arciform Design/Build

Chapter 3

p. 92 design, homeowner Stephanie Larrowe; furnishings, TOTeM
p. 95 interior design, Colleen Frederick, Studio Frederico; tiling, Hugh Frederick, Deco Stone & Tile
p. 96 design, Anne Palmer, Refresh Collections
p. 97 (top) design, homeowners Raymond and Dana Murphy
p. 97 (bottom) design, Joanne Palmisano; illustration, Cliff Deetjen
p. 99 design, Jane Coslick Designs and Restoration
p. 100 design, Joanne Palmisano
p. 101 design, Teresa Ridlon, Ridlon Interiors
p. 102 design, Michelle de la Vega; builder, Cady Construction
p. 103 (top) metal tables, Joel Hester, The Weld House
p. 103 (bottom) design, Joanne Palmisano
p. 104 design, homeowner Tawnya Pell
p. 105 design, Renee Tornabene, BulbtoBlossom.com

Chapter 4

p. 106 design, Annette Joseph
p. 108 photo by Joanne Palmisano
p. 109 design, Joanne Palmisano
p. 110 Arciform Design/Build
p. 111 (top) design, Renee Tornabene, Bulbto Blossom.com
p. 111 (bottom) photo by Joanne Palmisano
p. 112 design, Joanne Palmisano; illustration, Cliff Deetjen
p. 113 (left) design, homeowners Raymond and Dana Murphy; cabinetry, Simpson Cabinetry
p. 113 (right) photo by Joanne Palmisano
p. 114 (left) Arciform Design/Build
p. 114 (right) design, Joanne Palmisano, DIY Network Salvage Video Series
p. 115 design, homeowner Dana
p. 116 design, homeowner Kerri Hoyt-Pack
p. 117 design, Jane Coslick Designs and Restoration

Chapter 5

pp. 120–123 interiors, Rudolphe Faulcon; architect, Micheal Robinson
pp. 124–125 interior design, Kelly LaPlante; architect, Dan Smith, DSA Architects
pp. 126–127 design, Bamboo Revolution
p. 129 barn doors, Peter Pomerantz Woodworker
pp. 130–133 design, Atelier Ace, Creative Team
pp. 136–138 interior design, TruexCullins Architecture and Interior Design
pp. 139–143 interior design, Dominic and Patrick Coyne and Anne Quatrano, Square Feet Studio
pp. 144–147 design, homeowners Mike and Jackie Rice
pp. 148–151 interior design, Select Design
pp. 152–153interiors, Tracee Danyluk, Suri Iron, Jason Monfort; architect, Cory Omey; builder, Compound Construction
p. 158–159 interior design, Wilson and Associates; log table, Vermont Wildwoods

Chapter 6

p. 160 design, homeowner Kerri Hoyt-Pack, Anne DeWolf, and Arciform Design/Build
p. 162 design, Shannon Quimby, Shannon Quimby Design
pp. 164–168 design, homeowner Tricia Rose, Rough Linen
pp. 169–174 design, homeowners Rosanne Palmisano and Sean Roy; drawings, Melissa McCall Design; builder, David Lipkind
pp. 175–179 design, homeowner Kelly Giesen, Kelly G Design
pp. 180–183 design, homeowner Jennifer Siegal, Office of Mobile Design
pp. 184–189 design, homeowner Shannon Quimby, Shannon Quimby Design
pp. 190–195 design, Jane Coslick Designs and Restoration
pp. 196–200 design, homeowner Kerri Hoyt-Pack, Anne DeWolf, and Arciform Design/Build
pp. 201–203 design, homeowner Michelle de la Vega, Michelle de la Vega Design
pp. 204–209 design, homeowners Kim Clements, Joe Schneider, J.A.S. Design Build
pp. 210–213 design, homeowners Susan and Ryan Hayes; builder, Bill Litchfield, Specialty Design Vermont
pp. 214–217 design, homeowner, Jason Mathews, Sheridan + Company
pp. 218–223 design, homeowner Annie Haviland
pp. 224–227 design, homeowners Jessica Helgerson, Jessica Helgerson Interior Design; architect, Yianni Doulis
pp. 228–231 design, homeowners Terry and Teresa Hancock and Nathan Good Architects; builder, Tom Springer Construction

Chapter 7

throughout—designs, Joanne Palmisano; final project photography, Susan Teare; in-process photography, Joanne Palmisano
p. 232 design, Joanne Palmisano; illustration, Cliff Deetjen

Chapter 8

p. 262 interiors, homeowner Lori Scotnicki
p. 264 door design, homeowner and architect Tim Wybenga
p. 265 design, homeowners Dana and Raymond Murphy; cabinetry, Simpson Cabinetry; chalkboard, Vermont Farm Table
p. 266 interiors, homeowner Mary Atwood; cabinetry, George Ramos Woodworking
p. 268 design, Jane Coslick Designs and Restoration
p. 273 light by Andy Whitcomb, Whitcomb & Company
p. 276 Country Living Fair in Atlanta, The Little Art Studio booth
p. 277 collection of fish prints, homeowner Lori Scotnicki
p. 280 design, Joanne Palmisano; vases from Goodwill
pp. 280–281 Goodwill Industries of the Columbia Willamette: SE Portland, Oregon location

p. 281 (top right) Country Living Fair in Atlanta, Summerhouse booth
p. 282 Country Living Fair in Atlanta, Happy Chairs booth
p. 283 Country Living Fair in Atlanta, Rosa Bergen Antiques booth
p. 284 Country Living Fair in Atlanta, Rhine River Antiques booth
p. 285 Country Living Fair in Atlanta, The Dove Cote booth

Resources

p. 286 design, homeowner Renee Tornabene
p. 289 design, Joanne Palmisano; illustration, Cliff Deetjen